Also Available from Camphor Press

AMONG THE HEADHUNTERS OF FORMOSA

THROUGH FORMOSA

PROGRESSIVE FORMOSA

Progressive Formosa

by Hosoi Ryūtarō

camphor press

A Camphor Classic

Published by Camphor Press Ltd

83 Ducie Street, Manchester, M1 2JQ
United Kingdom

www.camphorpress.com

First published 1926. This edition

ISBN 978-1-78869-268-7 (paperback)
978-1-78869-269-4 (hardcover)

Set in 11 pt Linux Libertine

Contents

Foreword

In 1926 Taiwan – then called Formosa in the West – was Japan's model colony, an imperial showcase of the "benefits of enlightened Japanese rule". After two and half centuries of self-imposed isolation from the outside world, Japan began rapidly modernizing in 1868. In 1895 Japan defeated the ailing Qing dynasty in the first Sino-Japanese War, claiming Taiwan as its prize. In 1919 a civilian became head of the colonial government for the first time, signalling a transition from military rule which set Taiwan apart from the other major Japanese colony, Korea. Japan wanted to show that it deserved a seat at the table with the Western powers, and its governance of Taiwan was partially guided by that aim.

Progressive Formosa is government propaganda, plain and simple. It is written to show Japanese rule in the most positive light, with close attention paid to the markers of industrialization and "modernity". There are plenty of hard numbers to illustrate "progress": tonnage of materials produced, kilometers of railway track laid, numbers of hospitals built. This doesn't mean, however, that the book is uninteresting to the modern reader. With the benefit of hindsight and by knowing Japan's motives, readers gain a window into how the government of the time wished to be seen, and the things it wished to keep hidden.

The original 1926 edition is credited to the "Government of Formosa" but was in fact written by Hosoi Ryūtarō (細井柳太郎), an official from the Foreign Section of the Government-General of Taiwan. Hosoi was for a time the official English translator for the head of the island's colonial authorities and is mentioned (with the spelling "Hosui") by both Janet Montgomery-McGovern in her book *Among the Headhunters of Formosa* and by Owen Rutter in *Through Formosa*.[1] In this edition we credit the author fully for his work.

Hosoi discusses the ills Japan sought to combat, such as opium smoking and malaria, both of which were rampant in nineteenth-century Taiwan. Although the approach displayed in the book is paternalistic, the results were beneficial for the health of the people, with opium addiction greatly reduced through a system of licensing and treatment, and deaths from malaria cut to a fraction of previous rates.

Less positive are relations with the Indigenous people. The racist attitudes betrayed by writing of "civilizing" the "savages" point to underlying tensions which were to erupt shortly after the book was published. In 1930 the Seediq people of Musha (now "Wushe") revolted against their colonial rulers and were brutally crushed, with the Japanese deploying air raids, mustard gas, and artillery. When the smoke cleared, 644 Seediq were dead — along with 132 Japanese and two Han Taiwanese — and the illusion of benign rule was shattered.

It is the wider context that makes *Progressive Formosa* interesting to readers today. For example, the state-funded education previously open only to Japanese children had recently been extended to Taiwanese children, giving

1 Both titles provide wonderful insights into Taiwan under Japanese rule, and are available from Camphor Press.

those students more economic opportunities on leaving school but also providing the government with an opportunity to inculcate Japanese values. The "progress" of the book's title has a sting in the tail; and by understanding what the Japanese authorities thought of as desirable and progressive, we can understand how local cultures and identities in Taiwan were marginalized and suppressed.

Michael Cannings
March 2022

Preface

From the original 1926 edition

THREE full decades have now passed since Taiwan came into Japanese possession, and during this period it can be said without exaggeration that the island colony has made remarkable progress in economic, cultural and other directions.

As a result of this, commercial relations and communications with the homeland and foreign countries are becoming closer and closer with the passage of years, and an increasing number of visitors are constantly reaching the island.

The present prosperity and the bright prospects of Taiwan, coupled with its romantic history and its rich natural resources, are evidently attracting the attention of the cultivated public. Such being the case, it has been felt in many quarters that a book giving some general information regarding the various aspects of the island should be produced.

With the view of supplying this need, the Government has undertaken the publication of the work, which has been compiled by Mr. R. Hosui, until lately Chief of the Foreign Division.

As the present book is perhaps not sufficiently detailed

for those requiring special knowledge, it is contemplated to bring out an enlarged edition in the near future.

February, 1926

The Taiwan Government House

PROGRESSIVE FORMOSA

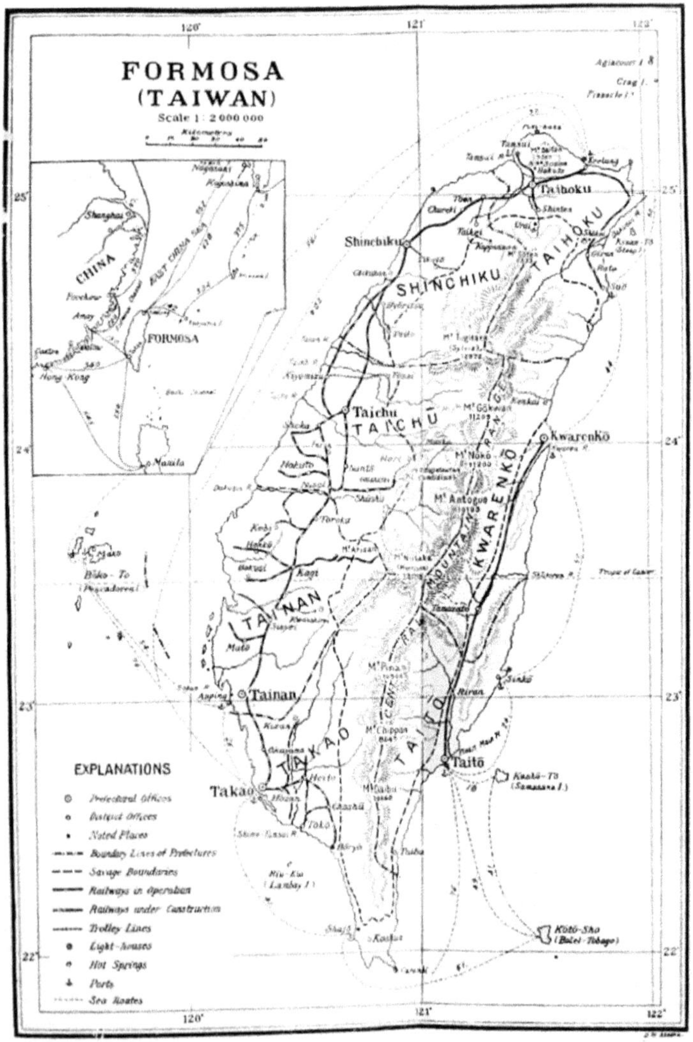

FORMOSA
(TAIWAN)
Scale 1: 2 000 000
CHINA
Shanghai
Foochow
Amoy
Hong Kong
EAST CHINA SEA
FORMOSA
Manila
Taihoku
Shinchiku
Taichu
Kwarenkō
Tainan
Takao
Taitō
TAIHOKU
SHINCHIKU
TAICHU
TAINAN
TAKAO
TAITŌ
KWARENKŌ
CENTRAL MOUNTAIN RANGE
Keelung
Tamsui
Anping
Kōtō-Sho (Botel-Tobago)
Kashō-Tō (Samasana I.)
Bōko-Tō (Pescadores)
EXPLANATIONS
Prefectural Offices
District Offices
Noted Places
Boundary Lines of Prefectures
Savage Boundaries
Railways in Operation
Railways under Construction
Trolley Lines
Light-houses
Hot Springs
Ports
Sea Routes
120°
121°
122°
25°
24°
23°
22°

I

Political History

THOUGH it is stated that the relations between Taiwan and China had their commencement in the early days of the seventh century A.D., yet historical records seem to indicate that it was after the advent of the Ming Dynasty that the island came under Chinese domination. In those days, when the Dutch occupied the southern part of the island and the Spaniards made invasion from the northern part, the island was in a chaotic condition, not having as yet been brought under the sway of any foreign country.

Meanwhile the Japanese had frequently been visiting the island with the view of opening up commercial relations with the islanders. In 1613, Harada Magoshichiro, a pioneer of foreign trade, came over to Taiwan, under instructions from Taiko Hideyoshi, demanding annual tribute, but this was declined on the pretext that there was no ruler in the island. In the following year, another Japanese pioneer, Naya Sukezaimon, made a large profit in Taiwan on his way home from the Philippine Islands. In 1615, Murayama Toan, a merchant of Nagasaki, made an audacious attempt to subjugate Taiwan, but he was defeated owing to the inadequacy of his forces.

In 1728, an adventurous pirate named Hamada Yahei, who had been greatly irritated against the Dutch because of the injustice with which they treated Japanese traders, set sail in a large vessel for Taiwan with the object of avenging the wrongs of his countrymen. Arriving at Anping, the Japanese expedition met with great difficulties; but the undaunted leader Yahei finally succeeded in taking captive the Dutch Governor Nuyts. Thus the claims and conditions proposed by the Japanese were accepted by the Dutch.

The relations between the island and the mainland are spoken as having commenced during the Sui Dynasty in the 17th century, but this is not asserted with any amount of accuracy. We shall therefore pass on to give a summary of the important events that have taken place since the inception of relations between Japan and Taiwan.

Before Taiwan came under Chinese rule, large numbers of Japanese adventurers, half pirates half traders, were attracted to Chinese waters, which afforded them vast and lucrative fields of adventure. The sea-faring Japanese folk made from time to time marauding expeditions along the Chinese coast and further sought fortune in the southern seas, usually making Taiwan their headquarters. The Japanese and Chinese pirates got along together well, owing to the bond of the mutual profit to be derived from their trading transactions. These pirates were divided into bands. The strongest of them was a band organized under the leadership of a Chinese called Gan Shi-sai. The crafty leader, on the strength of a previous visit to Japan, called himself "Japanese Kora," which means Japanese pirate-chief. Their piratical exploits on the Chinese coast now became so frequent that hardly any villages on the coast of Fokien and the neighbouring provinces escaped. Thus nearly the whole of the China and Taiwan trade was brought under their control.

The pirate-chief was succeeded by Ching Chi-lung, the father of Koxinga whose exploits rendered him one of the grandest figures in the history of Taiwan. Ching Chi-lung amassed enormous wealth and exercised almost unbounded influence over the trading rovers. With the express desire of making use of his wealth and power, the Ming Government offered him a position of high rank in the Province of Fokien, which he accepted, and together with his men acknowledged his allegiance to the Ming Dynasty. Taiwan was thus left for a time without any ruling power, and it was about this time that the Dutch and Spaniards commenced to establish themselves in Taiwan.

It was in 1603 that the Dutch occupied the Pescadores for a while, which action eventually led to their possession of Taiwan for a space of thirty-eight years (1624–1662). The Dutch settled as virtual rulers of the island.

They adopted a wise policy and made great efforts towards ameliorating the conditions of life of the inhabitants. “Fort Zeelandia” at Anping and “Fort Provintia” at Tainan are two strongholds constructed by the Dutch after they settled in the island. In September, 1662, the Dutch, after a heroic resistance continued for several months against the forces of Koxinga, were obliged to capitulate and leave Taiwan for good.

The great advantages enjoyed by other nationalities in Taiwan naturally attracted the envy of the Spaniards, who had established a trading station at Manila. In the beginning of 1626, a Spanish expedition occupied the point in the north known as Keelung, where they erected a fort which they named San Salvador. In 1629, the Spanish forces occupied Tamsui and built another substantial fort to which the name San Domingo was given. Then they set up a government; their missionaries commenced to convert the natives to Christianity, and a large share of merchandise was attracted to their well-financed colony;

indeed they saw their way to laying foundations for the eventual occupation of the island. These active efforts on the part of the Spaniards were considered by the Dutch authorities as detrimental to their trade and administration. And so they communicated the facts to the Government of Batavia, urging the necessity of sending an expedition to drive the rival colonists away. The Dutch made two successive attacks upon the Spanish fortresses, which, after weeks of desperate but futile operations, were at last forced to surrender in August, 1612, thus leaving the Dutch undisputed masters of Taiwan.

After a lapse of two decades, a great Chinese general came over to Taiwan and drove the Dutch out of the island. This was no other than the famous Koxinga himself. He was born of the Chinese pirate leader Ching Chi-lung and a Japanese woman, whose marriage took place at Hirado near Nagasaki.

When Koxinga attained his majority, the Tartar invasion occurred, which resulted in throwing the whole Chinese Empire into disorder and driving the Mings from the throne. In the early stages of the invasion, Koxinga's father continued loyally to oppose the Tartars, but eventually he accepted the overtures persistently made by them. Apparently entertaining apprehensions, however, regarding him, the Tartars carried Ching Chi-lung to Pekin, where he was made prisoner. But the brave Koxinga betook himself to flight, with plans in his mind for the complete extirpation of the Tartars. The invaders, now greatly enraged at his attitude, took revenge on his father by throwing him into a vile dungeon.

The young commander achieved brilliant victories in many battles fought with the Tartar; but finally he was deprived of provisions and reduced to great distress. His fond hopes being thus doomed to disappointment, he had to look about for safer headquarters. His attention was directed to the quiet and fertile island of Taiwan, and he commenced secret preparations with the hope of gaining the island for his own. The Chinese in Taiwan sent messages to Koxinga, inviting him to come over and free them from the Dutch.

Thereupon Koxinga collected loyal officers and soldiers who pledged their allegiance to his person and cause, and made immediate preparations for the expedition against the Dutch. The expedition called first at the Pescadores, where the plans were completed, and then the force landed in the north of Taiwan, when thousands of their countrymen received them with open arms and flocked to their banner.

When Koxinga arrived, the inhabitants of the whole island rose up against the Dutch, even the savages uniting with the Chinese, and all exulted at the immediate prospect of freedom. Koxinga's position now being secure, he sent messages to the Dutch forts, summoning the garrisons to surrender, intimating that refusal might cost them dear. The Dutch saw that they could no longer maintain their position, and abandoned Fort Provintia without a contest. Then the Dutch concentrated their forces at Zeelandia, hoisting over its fort the red flag of defiance. Koxinga ordered his artillery to storm the enemy's stronghold, but here they offered a tremendously stubborn resistance. Much annoyed at the obstinancy of his foe, Koxinga now instituted a close blockade, which proved effective.

Meanwhile the Dutch garrison made all possible efforts to obtain reinforcements and supplies from Batavia and to strengthen their position, but to little avail. When Koxinga had just completed the preparations for a general assault, the Dutch Governor Coyett sent a message declaring that he would hand over the fort upon conditions subject to Koxinga's consent. It was in the year 1662 that Dutch authority thus came to an end in Taiwan.

Now Koxinga found himself in complete possession of the island, and in fact gained supreme control of the China seas. He proclaimed himself King of Taiwan, and established his palace and court at Zeelandia, and at once appointed numerous civil and military officials in Taiwan and the Pescadores, placing his eldest son Cheng Ching-lung in command of the military and naval forces at Amoy. Chinese laws and customs and form of government were introduced, and Koxinga's time was devoted to the welfare of the island. Before embarking on the work of administration the new ruler made a tour of inspection throughout his domains. Wherever he went he never failed to treat the inhabitants with kindness and consideration, and he met with a warm welcome among his kinsmen everywhere that he appeared. The large stretches of fertile land lying waste impressed the new ruler more than anything else.

In order to consolidate his rule over the island, the first thing to be done was to provide the inhabitants with the necessaries of life. Agriculture was encouraged with such zeal that even the soldiers had to engage in this peaceful pursuit in their spare time. It was not strange that from this time onward, an unending stream of Chinese colonists continued to pour into the island, with the result that settlements sprang up in increasing numbers along the western coast.

Noting that Taiwan was fast growing strong and prosperous under his efficient administration and that his power and popularity were approaching their zenith, the ambitious ruler began, as might well be expected, to cast about for territorial aggrandizement. The Philippines, standing over against his domain, could not but prove an object of temptation to him. Koxinga had, as luck would have it, struck up a friendship with a Spanish Dominican friar, Riccio, about this time.

The shrewd ruler sent him to Manila as ambassador,

insistently demanding that the Spanish government should pay him a yearly tribute. The considerable number of Chinese then living in the capital had been informed of the existent state of affairs in Taiwan and of the object of the envoy's visit, and accordingly intense was their excitement over the matter.

The Spanish authorities, who clearly saw through the Chinese plans, suddenly opened a campaign against them with the result that the insurgents were nearly all killed. The Spaniards, however, allowed a certain number of tradesmen and merchants to escape the massacre, in view of the inconvenience they might suffer from the want of them.

On hearing of the incident from Riccio and a few kinsmen who barely escaped with their lives from Manila to Taiwan, Koxinga became furious, and at once set about organizing a large expedition, intent upon wreaking full vengeance on the Spaniards in Manila. At this momentous time, however, the great ruler was suddenly attacked by a dangerous illness which put an end to his ambitious plans. His death occurred in July 1662, at the early age of thirty-nine. Possessed of extraordinary courage, enterprise and ability, Koxinga carved out a kingdom for himself and provided a safe refuge for all loyal followers of the Ming Dynasty, while his life was devoted to restoration work for the lost empire. He was indeed one of the most wonderful characters recorded in the modern history of the Orient.

Soon after Koxinga passed away, his henchmen made Koxinga's brother Shu the second king of Taiwan in preference to his eldest son Cheng Ching, who had been disowned by his father because of his misconduct. In the meantime, the followers of the dead ruler at Amoy proclaimed Cheng Ching as the rightful heir to the throne.

About this time, it happened that the Tartar government, which had been eagerly watching an opportunity for dispersing the remnant of the adherents of the Ming Dynasty, combined with the Dutch, who had again appeared in the China seas, apparently with the intention of regaining Taiwan, in the common cause of driving the Ming Chinese from Amoy and Taiwan. Several battles were fought, but Cheng Ching was unsuccessful, and he retired to Taiwan with his family. Arriving in Taiwan, he was affectionately received by his uncle and declared the rightful successor to Koxinga.

With supreme responsibilities thrown upon him, Cheng Ching, now showed his loyalty to his father's cause by devoting all his energies to the welfare of his people and his land. During his reign many departments of industry, education and foreign commerce made remarkable progress. In 1682, Cheng Ching died at an early age, respected and honoured by all his subjects.

Ching Ko-tsang was the son selected by Cheng Ching to be his successor. But Cheng Ching's mother disclaimed him as her grandson, and so the second son Cheng Ko-Shewang was placed on the throne, only to have an uneasy career. The next year the Tartar government of Fokien attacked and occupied the Pescadores.

The young ruler, seeing no hope of success, had no alternative but to make unconditional surrender to the Tartar authorities. Thus after having been governed by the Koxinga family for a period of twenty-one years, the whole island passed under the Tartar rule.

Upon coming under the domination of the Tartar Government in 1643, the island was made a part of the province of Fokien. The name of Taiwan which was once given by the Dutch to one little isle was formally applied to the whole island. The capital was called Taiwan-fu, the seat of the central Government, and for administrative purposes the island was divided into three prefectures, namely, Taiwan, Shora and Hozan.

Appreciating the fact that the followers of Koxinga would not like to see their time-honoured system abruptly removed, the Tartar mandarins refrained from enforcing any drastic government measures upon the inhabitants. They did not allow their subordinate officers more than three years' service in the island, lest they should make common cause with the masses imbued with a propensity to rebellion. The Chinese Government apparently had no serious wish to civilize the island. Under such circumstances, it was no unusual thing that misrule and abuse prevailed to a notable extent, and unceasing troubles between the authorities and the people were the order of the day. Nothing worth recording had been accomplished during the period of their administration for two hundred years, until the Imperial Commissioner Liu Ming-chau assumed the reins of government in the island.

During this long span of years, more than a score of insurrections occurred, some of which were so formidable as to throw the entire island into tremendous convulsions. At times the mandarin authorities seemed utterly inefficient in meeting the situation before their eyes. In those days of confusion the official classes had a proverb, "Every three years an outbreak, every five years a rebellion."

A most significant feature of Taiwan history during this period was the never-ending stream of emigrants from the districts of South Fokien and North Kwangtung. With this tide of immigration, quite a large number of depraved characters drifted into the island and retired to the distant hills which were beyond reach of the stern arm of justice. The Chinese colonists at first settled on the western plains, but with the great increase of their numbers they spread towards the interior.

Their enterprise was met by a stout resistance on the part of the aborigines, the original occupants of the land. The simple and ignorant savages, however, proved no match for the Chinese who were distinguished for their industry, economy and craft. By force of arms and by means of crafty devices, their lands were gradually taken up and they were eventually forced to retire into the mountain jungles where they could live undisturbed. This entailed on the Chinese race the undying hatred of the savage tribesmen. In consequence, sanguinary struggles between the two races became so frequent that for more than two hundred years hardly a day passed without such an occurrence.

On the other hand, among the Chinese immigrants composed of different clans and classes, frequent quarrels and constant feuds prevailed. The Chinese Government made no serious efforts establish their supremacy in the island. They were practically engaged in hostilities, either with their own people or with the savages; while in later years different foreign nations were added to the number of their foes. Such a state of affairs won for the inhabitants the reputation of being a fierce and turbulent population.

In the meantime, however, agricultural and commercial industry made remarkable developments in the island, thanks to the energetic efforts of the hardworking settlers. The commercial possibilities and strategic importance of the island began to attract the attention of Western nations, which were now searching for fields of commercial expansion and colonial achievement.

From the time of the expulsion of the Dutch in 1662, up to the beginning of the nineteenth century there is no record of foreign intercourse with the island, with the single exception of Benyowsky's expedition. The history of this century is full of events connected with depredations and brutal atrocities committed on the part of the inhabitants, and with the dreadful sufferings of those strangers who were unfortunate enough to be cast on these inhospitable shores. Brief descriptions of some outstanding events will now be given in chronological order.

In 1771, Count de Benyowsky, a Hungarian adventurer, touched at the eastern shore of Taiwan on his way home from Kamtschatka. After killing a large number of the hostile savages who opposed his landing, the Count proceeded inland. Here he met a Spanish gentlemen named Don Hieronimo, who introduced him to Huapo, an independent chief of the country. He was received with much respect as a divine messenger, as being sent over to free their kinsmen from the Chinese yoke. Availing himself of the great friendship shown him by the chief, the Count conceived the idea of founding a colony on the island later on. But as he came to an untimely end, in Madagascar, while fighting against the French, his visionary scheme came to naught.

In 1842, the British ships *Nerbudda* and *Ann* were wrecked on the north coast of Taiwan and almost all of the crews were subjected to the most barbarous treatment and put to death by the Chinese.

As this incident happened immediately after the close of the war between England and China, great excitement was aroused all over the civilized world and particularly among the British. The British Minister in China at once took the case up, making forcible demands. The Chinese authorities barely succeeded in smoothing over the affair by humbly expressing their regrets at the horrible crime and by acceding to the demands put forward.

In 1867, the American vessel *Rover* became wrecked off the south coast of the island. The crew landed in order to find shelter, when they were swept down upon by the wild savages and brutally murdered to a man. On receiving news of the affair, the American Minister in Pekin promptly took steps to obtain redress from the Chinese Government. Though much time was spent in official procrastination, the Chinese authorities were not able to take any effective action regarding the matter. Thereupon, with the approval and assistance of the Chinese, the Americans conducted various expeditions into the savage district. Gallant and daring as their attempts were, the Americans did not meet with much success, except that they obtained mere promises from the chief of the particular tribesmen concerned that they would thenceforward extend shelter and assistance to foreign castaways. Even after this, however, many minor cases of the kind were reported around the coast of the island.

After a lapse of only a few years, it happened in the month of December, 1871, that a large fishing and trading ship belonging to the fishermen of Miyakojima, one of the Loochoo Archipelago, was wrecked on the southern coast of Taiwan, and fifty-four of the crew were brutally massacred by the Botan savages. A few survivors were eventually able to return to their homes, and through them the news of the disaster was made known to the Japanese authorities.

The Japanese sought redress from the Pekin government, but they as usual repudiated all responsibility. In 1873, a similar shipwreck incident occurred. This time, the Japanese government decided to take the matter of exacting a penalty into their own hands, not only for the benefit of the Japanese but also for that of the whole maritime world who suffered severely from the scourge.

In 1874, the Japanese expedition was organized, with Count Okuma as General Superintendent and General Saigo as Commander-in-Chief. Moreover, a number of American experts agreed to accompany the party in various capacities as they had unconcealed sympathies with the Japanese.

Just on the eve of the departure of the expedition, however, the American Minister suddenly came forward with a protest against the employment of any American ships or Americans, except on the condition that Japan should first obtain the written consent of China to the expedition. Notwithstanding the grave obstacles placed in their way, the Japanese government managed to send out the party as previously arranged. Landing at their destination, the expedition forces overcame the abominable Botan savages and penetrated far into the mountain fastnesses.

In the meantime a certain portion of the foreign community, as well as of the foreign press, were clamorously urging that Japan was availing herself of the troubles in Taiwan to wage war on China. As a matter of fact the approval and assistance lent by Americans to the course taken by Japan was regarded by the Chinese as a matter of the utmost consequence.

On receiving the news that the southern part of Taiwan was in the hands of the Japanese, the Chinese Government made preparations for sending a huge force of troops to the island. But as Japan had no ulterior object in view, and in fact desired a peaceful settlement of the dispute, the Government despatched Okubo Toshimitsu to Pekin as Special Commissioner. With the aid and intervention of the British Minister, Mr. Wade, afterwards Sir Thomas Wade, and the American Consul, General Le Gendre, the Japanese Government succeeded in concluding a peace agreement with China, the latter paying an adequate indemnity and giving assurance of better control over the savage tribes. The intelligent public came to appreciate the real motive underlying the action of Japan and gave ample credit to her for the good work she did in the interests of humanity.

At the close of the Franco-China war in 1884, Taiwan was demanded by France as a material security for the payment of an indemnity which the former power imposed upon the latter. In the month of August, the fortifications of Keelung were heavily bombarded and reduced to ruins by the French under Admiral Lespès and the French tricolour was planted on the spot.

In April of the following year, the French under Admiral Courbet captured the Pescadores after some slight bombardment. It is recorded that the Admiral was much impressed with the unique advantages of the harbour and strongly memorialized his government in favour of a permanent occupation of the islands. His effects, however, were of no avail, and on June 9th a Treaty providing for the evacuation of Taiwan and the Pescadores was signed. Two day later, the resourceful Admiral died of cholera, apparently aggravated by the disappointing turn of events. Thus the French operations which had continued for over nine months in the island came to an end.

Towards the middle of the nineteenth century, the leading countries of Europe and America began to turn their attention to Far Eastern shores, with the view of securing footholds there wherever trade prospects were promising. It is not to be wondered at, therefore, that the beautiful island of Taiwan, whose hidden riches had been fascinatingly talked about, attracted the wistful eyes of those countries. The British and then the Americans, Germans and French made propositions to gain domination over the island for trading purposes. But important domestic affairs withheld these nations from carrying out their plans of eastern colonization. Yet, as the foreign commerce of China developed, English and American vessels frequently called at Taiwan ports.

In 1860, two British firms established themselves in the island as general merchants. It was during the years 1858–1865, that Keelung, Tamsui, Takaw and Anping were thrown open to foreign residence and trade. In 1860, the British Government sent its first consular representative, Robert Swinhoe, to Taiwan.

In the years 1863–1865, the Chinese Maritime Customs

were opened in Tamsui, Takaw and Anping respectively, Englishmen being stationed in those cities as commissioners.

With the growth of commercial activity in the southern and northern ports, the arrival of foreign merchants and the establishment of mercantile agents in the island became a notable feature. The exports dealt in by the foreign traders consisted of rice, indigo, sugar, tea, camphor, coal, plant fibre, sulphur etc.

In those days, enterprising new-comers were exposed to no small amount of hardship and danger both by land and sea. On shore, the natives not infrequently gave exhibitions of their hostility to foreigners, while on the open seas numerous pirates plundered strange vessels.

The rights and privileges embodied in the treaties not being invariably respected, the foreign residents found themselves obliged to take the law into their own hands. Matters standing so, there were witnessed unceasing difficulties between the foreigners, the Chinese and the mandarin officials. During the year 1868, a crisis was reached when a serious disturbance broke out in connection with the camphor trade, accompanied by murderous attacks upon foreigners and the destruction of mission buildings.

Consequently Mr. Gibson, then British Consul, with the aid of a naval force, took military possession of Fort Zeelandia and Anping for a time. The affair was a great surprise to the Chinese authorities, and they immediately complied with the demands of the British authorities. As a result, peace and justice was secured for the foreign residents in the island.

As has been described above, the Japanese expedition in 1874 and the French campaign in 1884–1885 acted as great stimulants upon the mandarin authorities concerned with Taiwan. Indeed they now perceived how much of the world's attention was focused upon Taiwan, and in what a precarious position it was placed.

At this momentous time, two great mandarin officers came over to Taiwan in succession, under whose administration affairs in the island were invested with new life. The first officer, Shen Pao-chen, was sent in June, 1874, as Imperial Commissioner to take charge of the island and arrange defences calculated to prevent the Japanese from occupying the Chinese districts. The existent state of things in Taiwan convinced him of the necessity of introducing great reforms. He therefore submitted a memorial to the Pekin government recommending that thenceforward the island should be governed by a system adequate to its position and requirements, and that the viceroy of Fokien should be removed to this more important locality. Among the reforms he introduced, the following may be mentioned as matters of importance. Assumption of authority over the aborigines of the south, rearrangement of the administrative divisions, improvement of roads and defence works, utilization of foreign machinery in coal and oil mining, institution of an immigration office, and construction of the new capital, Taipeh.

It was when Taiwan had become the scene of war with the French that another hero, Liu Ming-chan, arrived in the island in 1884 as Imperial Commissioner to take command. The Chinese government, thoroughly awakened by the exigencies of the times, declared Taiwan an independent province in 1887, and appointed Liu Ming-chuan as the first governor. A thorough reorganization and redivision of the island was now effected, as a result of which the seat of the government was removed to the city of Taipeh.

In order to provide for the expense of the new and greatly enlarged administration, the new governor instituted a heavy taxation system which aroused a very marked opposition among the Chinese and foreign residents. The construction of modern forts of the best design was one of the most prominent innovations introduced on his initiative. Two cable lines were laid, between Anping and the Pescadores and between Tamsui and the Sharp Peak at the mouth of the Ming River in Fokien. Again, the telegraphic communication between Taipeh, Tainan, and Takow was now completed. With the view of promoting commerce and peace, the governor formed plans for building a railway from north to south, improving the harbour of Keelung and opening up roads into the country districts.

Seeing that no advance had been made in gaining control over the hill-tribes, Liu Ming-chuan announced his intention of civilizing the savages and opening their country to Chinese trade. Following what he considered to be a just and reasonable plan, he made great efforts, but after all his policy did not obtain any success. In June, 1891, Governor Liu left the island on account of ill health. After his departure from the island up to the time of the Japanese occupation scarcely a month elapsed without finding the Chinese engaged in warfare with the savages along the disputed border.

Liu Ming-chuan, whatever may be said against him, must be acknowledged to have been an intelligent, liberal-minded and progressive person.

His successor, Shao Yu-lien, tried to win popularity among the islanders by extensive economies, but the new incumbent of the post had not the capacity necessary for carrying out the progressive plans of his illustrious predecessor. In October, 1894, Shao turned over the charge of the island to Tang Chin-sung, who proved to be the last officer under the Chinese régime to hold office.

Meanwhile a new centre of disturbance was created in Korea, which at last led to the outbreak of war between

China and Japan. The following year hostilities came to an end and a Treaty of Peace was signed in April, by which Taiwan was ceded in perpetuity to Japan.

The resident Chinese, however, proclaimed a republic and offered resistance to the newcomers. It was not until the end of October 1895 that the quasi-republicans were completely conquered, the last stand being made in the south by Liu Yung-fu, the Black Flag Chief who distinguished himself during the French war in Annam.

Even after this, the country districts were found to be infested by innumerable bands of outlaws and brigands, who obstinately resisted for many years the Japanese attempts to round them up. The Japanese government, invested with complete control as well as with civil administrative powers, finally succeeded in pacifying the island and in placing it on the high road to progress and prosperity.

A Modern Street in Taihoku

2

Geographical Description

FORMOSA or Taiwan consists of Taiwan proper, the Pescadores and many smaller islands; these all lie between the parallels of 210° 45’ and 250° 38’ North Latitude and between the meridians of 119° 18’ and 122° 6’ East Longitude of Greenwich.

Taiwan is separated from South China by a channel about one hundred miles in width, and faces towards the Pacific on the East and the Philippines and Hongkong on the South-west. The island is approximately 240 miles long from north to south and 90 miles wide at the widest part, with a circumference of 708 miles. It covers an area of 13,807 square miles, being a little larger than Holland and a trifle smaller than Switzerland. The island is oblong in shape like the leaf of a tree, stretching from north to south.

A chain of mountains traverses the island lengthwise which forms a kind of back-bone, dividing it sharply into two distinct parts. The eastern half is exceedingly steep and craggy, while the western part is flat and fertile. On the northern part of the east coast, a continuous range of high cliffs projects for about twenty-five miles, to a height of 6,000 feet, presenting a perpendicular face to the sea.

These were described by Mr. Guillemard, an English naturalist, as the highest and most magnificent cliffs known in the world. It might therefore be imagined that at some earlier period the island may have been much larger: that continuous undermining by the sea may have caused a gigantic landslip in which many hundreds of square miles had simply slid off into the mighty Pacific.

As seen from a distance, the outline of the mountains clad in brilliant verdure is at once beautiful and fantastic; and to this Taiwan is indebted for its European appellation of "Ilha Formosa" (Beautiful Isle) bestowed by the Portuguese navigators early in the sixteenth century.

The western part of the island, sloping gently with its alluvial plains to the sea, has largely been brought under cultivation, affording remarkable possibilities for the development of commerce and industry.

In the central mountain range, there tower up a number of peaks attaining no inconsiderable elevation. The loftiest in the north is Mt. Sylvia, soaring 12,972 feet in altitude. In the south, Mt. Morrison or Niitakayama, with a height of 13,075 feet, is the sovereign peak, being the very highest in the entire territory of Japan.

Thus the greater portion, say two-thirds, of the island is covered with mountains and upland country. In the midst of these rugged scenes, the savage aborigines, the oldest known inhabitants of the island, have their homes. The entire western plain and a portion of the eastern coast are inhabited by Japanese and Formosans. In the mountainous regions, there lie imprisoned immense natural resources that wait for exploitation. Owing to its geographical formation, there are no quiet peaceful rivers to be seen in the island. All the streams, whether large or small, partake more of the nature of mountain torrents, their channels taking prodigious curves in one direction and another.

When the typhoon season arrives, these rivers suddenly

rise and frequently play havoc with property. The two large rivers are the Dakusuikei and the Shimo Tamsuikei, measuring 97 and 90 miles in length respectively.

Climate

As Taiwan extends into both the tropical and sub-tropical zones, with the Tropic of Cancer passing through its centre near Kagi, the island possesses varying climates. The climate is, on the whole, agreeable and healthy, being tempered by the influence both of the sea current and the monsoons. The summer is long, though not accompanied by unbearable heat; while the winter is short and no severe cold is known. Snow is very seldom experienced on the levels, though the summits of its lofty mountains remain crowned with snow for a short period during the winter.

For the reader's information, we here quote the average mean temperatures in January and July as recorded in the three chief cities for the period from 1901 to 1920 inclusive.

	Taihoku	Taichu	Tainan
January	50° 18	60° 8	62° 24
July	82° 4	81° 68	81° 86

The dry and the rainy seasons occur in the north and in the south at exactly opposite times. In the north, the rainy season lasts from October to March, the weather being generally depressing, with cold drizzling rains, broken now and then by a spell of pleasant days. During these months the south takes its pleasure, enjoying a continual round of fine, delightful weather that leaves nothing to be desired. The rainy months in the south are characterized by frequent thunderstorms, causing the tremendous rainfalls peculiar to the tropics.

The atmosphere thus cooled and purified creates an inexpressibly refreshing sensation. One striking feature of the Formosan climate is the visitation of the great winds or typhoons, as they are called, which are decidedly not pleasant. They never occur before May or later than November, while August and September are the most likely months. There have been recorded in Formosa three or four typhoons each year, though only one storm as a rule is really severe. A fierce typhoon often causes as disastrous damages to crops, property and life.

A Formosan Family

As has been described above, Taiwan, as far as its vertical contour is concerned, may be divided into three parts, the mountains proper, the broad western slope with its alluvial and fertile plains and the narrow eastern slope terminating in a high and precipitous coast. The island possesses a variety of climes, frigid, temperate, sub-tropical and tropical, due to the varying altitudes.

The soil is amazingly fertile almost all over the island and profuse displays of Nature are found in all directions.

Under these exceptionally favourable conditions, it is no wonder that all over the island plant and animal life flourishes in great luxuriance and variety.

3

Inhabitants and Population

THE first census-taking throughout the Japanese Empire was carried out only as recently as October 1st, 1920; whereas in the colony of Taiwan, a census of the population has been made three times, including the 1920 general census, the first taking place in 1905 and the second in 1915.

From a racial point of view, the inhabitants of the island may be divided into three groups: Japanese, Formosans and foreigners. The Formosans may be divided into two classes viz. the Hans and aborigines. The Hans are again subdivided into two groups, according to the provinces in China from which they originally emigrated. These are Kwangtung and Fukien. The Haklos were earlier settlers from Fukien province, and being refugees of the Ming period, are mild and law-abiding. The Hakkas who later emigrated from Kwangtung province, a hardy and industrious race, took up their residence in the savage border districts. In early days, they had frequent conflicts with the aborigines. According to the latest census returns, nearly 95 percent of the entire inhabitants are islanders of the Han race.

The aborigines are partly a savage and warlike people

known as head-hunters. They are of Malayan extraction. Apparently, they conceive themselves to be the owners of the island, and regard the rest as invaders, by whom they have been gradually driven back into the mountain recesses. They get their living by hunting, fishing, and farming. Those aborigines who live on the plains and who have come under the civilizing influence of the Chinese are called the Juku-Ban or sinicized aborigines. These people are now being given facilities for receiving education and acquiring a knowledge of useful trades.

The following are the returns of population as at the end of 1923.

	Male	Female	Total
Japanese	100,886	80,961	181,847
Formosans	1,883,715	1,795,656	3,679,371
Aborigines	42,180	41,997	84,177
Foreigners	23,489	7,214	30,703
Total			3,976,098

The average density of population in Taiwan per square mile is over 287.3.

4

Administration

ON the 17th of April, 1895, the island of Taiwan was ceded by China to Japan as a result of the Peace Treaty of Shimonoseki. From that date till the end of September, 1919, the island has been under the rule of eight successive Governor-Generals, all military or naval men, assisted by seven successive Chiefs of Administration, many reforms having during these years been introduced into the government organization. On the 1st of October, 1919, Baron Den, a civilian statesman, was appointed Governor-General of Taiwan in succession to General Akashi, who died in office. This event marks an important epoch-making era in the history of the government of Formosa. On assuming his duty as Governor-General, Baron Den carried out a sweeping reform of the administration system quite unprecedented in the annals of the island's history, diminishing the influence of the centralization system in favour of a system of local self-government.

The Government General of Formosa constitutes, as its title signifies, the supreme machinery of government in the island, which is administered by a Governor General, assisted by a director-general who manages the general administrative business. The present Governor General is H. E. Takio Izawa and the Director General of Administration is Mr. Fumio Goto. The Government General consists of the Governor General's Secretariat and four Departments: Internal Affairs, Finance, Productive Industries, and Police.

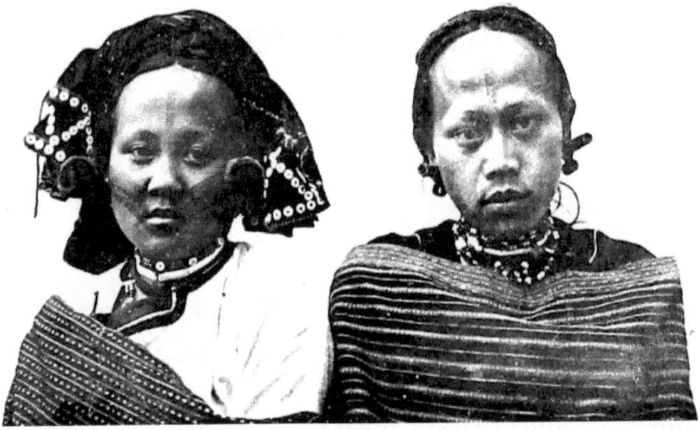

Savage Man and Woman

Besides these there are special establishments, namely, the Monopoly Bureau, the Communications Department, the General Research Institute and the Customs. These Offices attend to all the government business that falls within their respective spheres.

For administrative purposes, the whole island is divided into five provinces and two *cho*. In the western part of the island where the population is thickly distributed and where the standard of civilization is advanced, there are established five provincial governments, in Taihoku, Shinchiku, Taichu, Tainan, and Takao, each province being placed under a governor. The eastern part, comprising sparsely populated districts and backward in civilization, is divided into two *cho*, (*cho* is a little lower than a province), viz. Taito and Karenko, each having a governor. The five provinces are divided up into five municipalities, forty-seven districts (*gun*), and two hundred and sixty towns (*gai*) and villages (*sho*). The two *cho* are subdivided into seven sub-*cho*, two towns, one village, and nineteen *ku*.

In each province, municipality, town and village, there is established a consultative council, the members of which body are appointed from among the leading people resident in the locality.

To the Government General of Taiwan, there is attached the Government Council, a supreme advisory body, whose members are nominated by the Governor General. The function of this council is to give expression to public opinion with regard to problems of government on which it is consulted.

In March, 1896, the military administration was superseded by a civil administration. In view of the peculiar circumstances in which Taiwan stands, the Imperial Government authorities found it necessary to empower the Governor General of Taiwan to issue ordinances having the force of law. With the approval of the Diet, on March 30th of the same year, the Imperial Government promulgated a law (No. 63) to the above effect. As it was clearly provided for in the law that it should become invalid after a period of full three years from the date of its coming into force, approval was obtained for its further continuance in the 13th, the 16th, and the 21st sessions of the Imperial Diet. In January, 1909, another law (No. 31) was passed, in the 22nd session of the Diet, extending its period of validity from three to five years. In the 27th and the 37th sessions, the further continuance of the said law was again approved. And finally in the 44th session, approval was given to the promulgation of a new law (No. 3, 1921), which is in force at the present time.

It may be of interest to outline certain important points

of difference between the law in force on the one hand, and the laws Nos. 63 (1896) and 31 (1909) on the other. Up to the time of the promulgation of law No. 3 (1921) all matters that had to be ordained as laws in Taiwan were as a rule promulgated in the form of an ordinance by the Governor General, and only those particular laws of Japan that were considered to be conveniently applicable to the Island colony were added by Imperial order. The new law No. 3 (1921) reversed this principle – enforcing home laws in Taiwan by Imperial ordinance, and promulgating under the Governor General's ordinance only such laws as have to be made fit for Taiwan in virtue of its special conditions. Formerly, the period of validity of the law was limited to three or five years, but now this usage has completely been done away with.

Residence of the Governor-General

Judicial System

The law courts in Taiwan are under the direct control of the Governor General, and are constituted by the Formosan Government Court Regulations, which place them on a district basis from the courts of Japan proper. The judiciary consists of one supreme court and three local courts. The supreme court is divided into the court of review and the court of appeal. In the local courts a single judge is competent to discharge judicial functions; but certain specific cases have to be heard and tried before a collegiate court composed of three judges. With the exception of such matters as fall within the original jurisdiction of the appeal department of the supreme court, the local court deals with the trial on first instance of civil and criminal cases occurring within its jurisdiction, and also attends to matters relating to preliminary examinations in criminal and non-contentious cases.

The Review Department of the Supreme Court deals with cases on appeal from the decisions of local courts, on the hearing of which appeals three judges are required to sit. In the Appeal Department of the Supreme Court, five judges sit to try cases. This Department deals with appeals from the decisions of the Review Department, offences respecting the Imperial house, internal disturbances, foreign invasion, diplomatic relations, and those offences specified in the Brigandage Penal Regulation etc.

There is at present one supreme court in the capital, Taihoku, and three local courts are established at Taihoku, Taichu and Tainan. Branches of local courts are also established in three localities.

Registration and Notary Public Offices, which are under the control of the local courts, have been opened in twenty-nine important centres.

Police System

In consequence of the great local administration reorganization effected in September, 1920, as referred to in a foregoing chapter, a Police Department was installed in each provincial Government, an administrative official being appointed as its director.

In each district office (*gun*) there was instituted a police section with a police inspector or police sergeant as its chief, thus conferring upon a district governor power to supervise police administration. A police section was simultaneously established in each *cho*, having a police inspector as its chief. Under each *cho* are placed a number of sub-*cho*, with police inspectors and police sergeants as their heads, who also part in the administrative affairs of the *cho* and assist the government of *cho* in their official duties.

Besides this, in Taihoku, Taichu, Tainan, Keelung, and Takao, which have been organized as municipalities, there are established police offices, with branches in important districts of these cities.

In the Government General, there is a Police Department, which is invested with the supervision of local police organizations, and has under its efficient control the police administration throughout the island.

With a view of avoiding all immediate intervention on the part of the Police Department authorities in active police functions, as was previously the case, the Department staffs have largely been reconstituted from among civil officials instead of police officials, with the exception of the Aboriginal Affairs Section.

The Hoko System or Auxiliary Police Organization

Among the existing organizations for the maintenance of peace and order in the island, a matter worthy of special mention is the Hoko system. This system is a self-governing police institution originally planned and developed under the régime of the Chinese Ming Dynasty. In appreciation of the efficient and remarkable service it rendered, the Japanese Government, on taking possession of the island, issued regulations for the adoption of the system with the necessary modifications. According to these regulations, one Ko consists of ten households, and ten of these groups constitutes one Ho division. The heads of these groups and divisions are elected from among the village or town elders, as the case may be. Those who are so elected take up their duties with the sanction of the provincial and sub-provincial governors. These positions are purely honorary and no renumeration is given. In normal times, their functions consist in preserving the peace and order of the neighbourhood, in keeping records of the houses and population in their respective districts, maintaining a high standard of public morality and welfare among the young men, and in making the people acquainted with all new laws and regulations as they come out.

The Kentenji Chinese Temple

In a word, all the members are jointly held responsible for occurrences taking place within their respective spheres of activity. The Hoko is further required to maintain a volunteer corps made up of able-bodied males from seventeen to fifty years of age, all well-conducted men. These men are chosen from one or several Ho divisions at the rate of ten men from each division. The corps is under the control of the local police. The volunteers receive no stated pay for their services, but are supplied with board.

The volunteer corps have to be constantly prepared against every emergency and any calamity that may endanger their fellow-people's safety, lives and property. As may be gathered from the above, the system in question is really a characteristic and admirable organization that promises to become a highly useful autonomous police fit for the requirements of civilized peoples.

5

Religion and Education

Religion

IN the chronological order of their introduction into Taiwan, the forms of religion prevailing in the island may be divided into (1) those which existed before the Japanese occupation and (2) those which have been subsequently introduced. Among the religions that had been propagated before the island passed into Japanese possession, Confucianism, Taoism, Buddhism and Christianity may be counted as important. Above all, Taoism and Saikyo, a form of religion combining in its doctrine and practice Buddhism and Taoism, exercised a predominant influence over the island population.

Christianity was first introduced into the southern part of Taiwan as early as 1627 by a Dutch missionary, Georgius Candidius, and in the following year Spanish friars, with Father Francisco Mola as head, brought over the same faith to the northern part.

Protestantism was introduced into the southern part in 1865 by Dr. Maxwell of the English Presbyterian Mission and to the northern part by Dr. Mackay of the Canadian Presbyterian Mission in 1872.

The religions that have since found their way to the island are Japanese Shintoism, Buddhism as developed in

Japan and various Christian denominations brought over by Japanese missionaries. These forms of religion prevail largely among Japanese settlers, though no small number of converts are found among Formosans nowadays.

There is a tendency for religious work among the Formosans to be almost entirely left in the hands of European missionaries. The Christian Churches established in Taiwan by Japanese effort include the Japanese Presbyterian Church, the Episcopal and the Greek Catholic Church.

In Taiwan as in Japan proper, there is more than one Shinto Shrine dedicated to National Kami in important places where many Japanese are settled.

Strictly speaking, worship at the shrines or Jinja, as they are called, has nothing to do with religious worship. The leading one of these is the Taiwan Jinja in Taihoku. It is a National Shrine, consecrated to the memory of the late Prince Kitashirakawa who died during the expedition to Taiwan in 1895, and three other Japanese deities. Religion is hardly to be found among the aboriginal tribes. Worship of the Sun and Ancestors, of a most primitive fashion, prevails among them.

Education

Up to a few years ago, Japanese and Formosan children had to be instructed separately under different systems, owing to the difference of language and mode of living. In view of the remarkable improvement made by the Formosan people in manners and in the Japanese language, however, the Government authorities introduced a coeducational system in April 1920, tentatively admitting promising and successful Formosan children into some Japanese schools. The result was very satisfactory, and fully convinced the Government that the time was ripe for radically re-shaping the existing system of education.

The Taiwan Jinsha

In February 1922, the New Educational Law of Taiwan was promulgated as an Imperial ordinance (No. 20), providing that all grades of secondary schools shall be equally thrown open to all Japanese and Formosan boys and girls without distinction, and, with regard to elementary education, that those who speak Japanese as the language of daily life shall be admitted into elementary schools and that those who do not speak Japanese sufficiently well shall enter public schools. Discrimination in educational opportunities between the two races has been completely eliminated, so that this period may well be called an epoch-making era in the history of civilization in Taiwan.

In April, 1924, there were 132 elementary schools and 720 public schools throughout the island; and the number of pupils was 24,221 and 240,543 respectively. The percentage of Japanese children attending school was 97.63 while that of Formosan children was 32.34. The percentage in the latter case is insignificant, yet as compared with that of five years before, namely 20.69, one cannot but be surprised at the very rapid strides made in such a short period of years.

The New Educational Law provides that, excepting the public schools and normal schools intended for those who are not able to receive instruction in Japanese, the educational system as enforced in Japan proper shall be pursued in Taiwan. As a consequence, all the public high schools, girls public high and professional schools primarily provided for Formosans have been converted respectively into Secondary Schools, girls' high schools and special schools. They have all been reorganized in conformity with the educational law, and are thrown open equally to both Japanese and Formosans.

According to the figures taken in April, 1924, there were twenty middle grade schools with a total number of 6,478 students; four technical schools with 1,413 Sanitation and Hygiene students altogether; three normal schools with 1,926 students; one high school of the seven years' course with 160 students; four special schools, namely, one higher commercial school, one higher agricultural and forestry schools, one special commercial school and one medical school, with an aggregate number of 84 students.

The Government have been and are making earnest efforts in the direction of providing education for the youthful aboriginal people. In April, 1922, there were 32 public schools exclusively established for the hill-tribe children, with 5,264 pupils.

Besides, there were 167 smaller schools of a lower grade placed under the care of police, the number of attendances totalling 4,015. After completing with honours their studies in these schools, three young men entered and graduated from the Special Medical School and are now practising medicine, and some are engaged in school and government service after having finished the course provided by the government schools. As can be inferred from the above, some of these young men are found to be remarkable bright and successful. They are undoubtedly possessed of the capability of undertaking any profession or art.

School for Tribesmen's Children

6

Sanitation and Hygiene

When the Japanese arrived in Taiwan, the first question that pressingly called for their attention was the immediate improvement of sanitary conditions. In those days, all towns and villages were found in a simply unhealthy and filthy condition: all possible kinds of epidemic and endemic diseases scourged the island through its length and breadth. In the face of this dreadful state of things, the ignorant people remained helpless, not being able to take any active measures for insuring public health.

Accordingly the authorities have unceasingly exerted their endeavours towards effecting such sanitary improvement as they considered necessary for meeting the situation. Their efforts have now proved fruitful and the whole island is transformed into a surprisingly healthy and delightful country.

There are at present twelve civil hospitals in important places, cities and towns, all being placed under the direct control of the Government General. Of these the largest and best-equipped is the Taihoku Hospital, the buildings and equipments of which cost approximately 3,000,000 yen. This is regarded as the most magnificent and commodious establishment of the kind in the Far East. Besides these government hospitals, there are 18 local public hospitals and 68 private ones. In out-of-the way localities where people cannot gain access to hospitals, nearly 145 public medical officers are stationed for the benefit of the country people. In addition to these, there are a large number of medical practitioners scattered over the island, the greater portion of them being Formosans.

With the view of checking all the infectious diseases that have for long menaced the population, the authorities elaborated various preventive agencies. And these agencies under the able and efficient management of the proper authorities have accomplished a highly successful achievement. The most dreaded plague was completely stamped out in 1917, and the endemic malarial fever that used to exact a heavy toll of life, has now been practically suppressed, so that nowadays, hardly any cases are found in towns and cities.

It is encouraging to note that the Formosans are rapidly becoming alive to the efficacy of modern medicine and sanitary measures. In many of the principal towns, the government and municipal authorities are endeavouring in cooperation, to establish modern sanitary developments, among which may be mentioned the construction of waterworks, sewerage systems, housing, street improvement, establishment of recuperative resorts, reconstruction of slaughter-houses, cemeteries, crematories and the control of food and drinks.

It may be added that on these lines of public health work, the authorities are bent on prosecuting their studies and researches, so that the people in the colony may be able to enjoy a healthy and comfortable life. Last but not least, we should reckon to the credit of the government of Taiwan its opium control policy. On their arrival in Taiwan, the Japanese found themselves faced with a problem as to what course should be pursued in regard to the smoking of opium, to which habit a surprisingly large proportion of Formosans were hopelessly addicted.

The Government, in accordance with Baron Goto's advice, adopted a system of gradual suppression, with an eventual prohibition of opium smoking. This wise and far-sighted policy has turned out remarkably successful. The number of licensed smokers has steadily fallen off year after year, indicating that the object aimed at can be accomplished at no distant future.

Taihoku Hospital

7

Communications and Transport

WHILE Taiwan remained a Chinese territory, it possessed no good natural harbours. Tamsui and Anping, two well-known ports in those days, were not capable of accommodating ships of any size, owing to a troublesome bar in both places. Takao was even less accessible, being merely an open roadstead. The business of carrying by sea was limited to traffic between these ports and South China ports, and it was carried out by the small boats of the Douglas Steamship Company, and by Chinese junks.

Since the arrival here of the Japanese, the sea routes have undergone a great transformation. Marine transport in Taiwan is now conducted chiefly by the Osaka Shosen Kaisha with aid of the Government of Taiwan. The Yamashita Kisen Kaisha has recently participated in the shipping business of the island.

The subsidized line service was originally started between Japan proper and Taiwan. With the subsequent progress of the Island and its increased connections with the outside world, the subsidized services have been extended so as comprise the following routes:

- the Keelung–Kobe Line (N.Y.K.) the Takao–Yokohama Line (N.Y.K.)
- the Coast Service Line (O.S.K.)
- Takao–Tientsin Line (O.S.K.)
- Takao–Hongkong Line (O.S.K.)
- Keelung–Saigon–Bangkok–Singapore Line (O.S.K.)
- Keelung–Takao–Manila–Sandakan–Batavia–Semarang Line (O.S.K.)
- the Keelung–Hongkong–Haiphong Line (Y.K.K.)

At present six steamers of 6,000 to 10,000 tons are run on the Kobe–Keelung Line, each making two trips a month from each terminus, whilst three or more steamships are run on the other lines. Upon the completion of the harbour improvement works now in course of progress both at Keelung and Takao, these lines will assume still greater activity and importance.

Roads and Railways

When the Japanese came to this island, the first thing that surprised them was a dire absence of communication facilities, there being nothing worth calling a road. There were paths leading from village to village; there were some country roads connecting towns with the surrounding villages. In some of the sugar districts there were roads which were used by buffalo carts transporting sugar cane. Consequently travel, other than on foot or by chair, was impossible. During the Chinese régime little attention was given to the matter of opening and improving roads. As a matter of fact, any such thing was left in the hands of rich families.

The present highway running from north to south along the western coast is but an extension of the work initiated by the Japanese expeditionary army, which found it imperative to open up a pathway for its advance. Indeed, they may be said to have been the first road makers in the island. Nowadays in many districts there are found fine and wide roads, available for the passage of carts. With the subsequent settlement of affairs throughout Taiwan, a period of administrative activity dawned upon the island. The authorities formed plans of projecting public road facilities, not only to establish connections between important places, but also to give access to remote districts which had been sufficiently developed to warrant road-making or where intensive industries had sprung up. The cost of road construction is met by voluntary contributions and local taxation, and in many cases the work is carried out by the aid of statute labour. The extended mileage of roads built and opened to traffic up to the end of 1921 was approximately 8750 miles.

Wire Suspension Bridge

Efforts are also being made to open up pathways in the savage regions, and to make transverse roads across the central mountains. For this purpose, tunnelling, levelling and bridge-spanning work is in process of being carried on in many directions.

It will, however, be a long time before a network of fine and well-kept roads suited for all kinds of traffic will be found in existence in the island.

Railways

Prior to the Japanese occupation, the railway facilities in the island were, as might well be expected, extremely deficient. There was only one solitary railway of an old type some 62 miles in length, running between Keelung and Shinchiku. It was in every detail in so wretched a condition that a satisfactory train service was out of the question, the rolling stock being limited, and entirely unsuited to the requirements.

Consequently, the old line was completely reconstructed by the Japanese authorities so as to avoid the numerous short curves and sharp gradients. In 1899, the project of building the trunk railway line between Keelung and Takao was launched. After ten years' hard work, the main line, totalling 247 miles length, was completed, thus bringing the northern and southern extremities of the island into direct communication.

It has on its route such important cities as Taihoku, Taichu and Tainan, and traverses the central districts yielding the island's staple products: tea, rice, and sugar. While largely contributing in this way to the economic and industrial development of the country, the line forms a main artery of passenger and freight traffic.

With a view to affording as great facilities as possible to public traffic and transport, the Government are sparing no efforts in the matter of constructing new railways on important routes and of improving old ones.

In the meantime, the Government are encouraging

private individuals and firms to push forward railway construction on the terms of a Government guarantee of a certain amount of profit for a period of ten years dating from the commencement of the operation of the railway, and by furnishing any necessary subsidies. The other branch lines in operation are the Tamsui–Taihoku line and the Takao–Heito line.

The Keelung–Giran line is now completed and the Karenko–Taito line is in course of construction, though a considerable portion of the latter is already open to traffic. The total mileage of the government lines at the end of 1922–1923 fiscal year was 477.8 miles.

Beside the government railways, there are private district railways, extending over 300 miles, which are under the management of the sugar manufacturing companies, and used largely for cane transport purposes and partly for general traffic.

Push Cars

As auxiliary means of transport, there are numerous light trolleys in various parts of the island, a characteristic feature of Taiwan. These are well linked np with other railway lines. The aggregate mileage of the push-car lines is 586 miles.

The Arisan Railway

This chapter would be incomplete without a reference to the Arisan Railway. This line, covering a distance of more than 54 miles, is under the management of the Industrial Department. This railway is exclusively designed for the conveyance of lumber from Mt. Arisan, but the public may be permitted to travel by it. As the railway crawls up round the rugged mountains, there are found along the line sixty-eight tunnels, three spiral sections, and many switch-backs.

The magnificent kaleidoscopic views which passengers enjoy as they ascend to the Arisan forests, 8,000 feet above sea-level, are simply wonderful, and must be seen to be appreciated.

8

Public Works

At the time Taiwan came under Japanese rule, among the things which engaged the attention of the government authorities as being the most important and pressing for the welfare and development of the island were the public works.

In view of this the authorities have carried out works of street improvement, water supply, sewerage system and river improvement, and have constructed hospitals, schools and many other public institutions.

In a word, they have left no stone unturned to make necessary provision for sanitary, educational, and industrial development. Thanks to the wise and energetic efforts of the authorities concerned, the leading cities of the island have acquired in many respects the equipment appropriate to modern civilized cities. As reference has been made to these subjects in the foregoing chapters, we may here confine ourselves to an outline of the harbour construction and electrical enterprises.

The commencement of electrical enterprise in the island dates as far back as 1902, when leading Japanese business men formed a joint-stock company with the object of supplying electric light to Taihoku city, utilizing the flow of the Shinten-Kei River. But in view of the fact that the various industries which had then been developed stood much in need of an abundant supply of electric power, the Government conceived the scheme of taking up and managing the electric business for itself. As an outcome of the plan, in the ensuing years, an Electric Works Office was established.

The total output of electric power brought under the direct management of the office amounted to 11,200 h.p., obtained in the northern, central and southern part.

In August, 1919, a company with a capital of 30,000,000 yen was founded under Government auspices with the title of the Taiwan Denryoku Kaisha (the Taiwan Electric Power Company). Thenceforward all the electric and gas works were made over to the newly established company. The company is engaged on the work of constructing colossal power plants at Lake Jitsu-getsutan or Lake Candidius, situated on the boundary of the central mountain range in Taichu Province, with the plan of obtaining 140,000 h.p. from the water of the lake. Though the progress of the works has to some extent been delayed by the world-wide financial depression, their completion is anticipated with certainty in the course of a few years. When the projected electric works begin to operate in full swing, it will not fail to have a great and far-reaching effect on the economic development of the island. The latest inquiry shows that the Company can already furnish 13,362 electrical horse power.

In addition to this enterprise, there are seven other power companies in the island, with an aggregate capacity of 23,548 k.w.

Harbour Construction

Its coast line lacking in indentations, the island of Taiwan is not favoured with natural havens of shelter from the surging waves of the open sea. The eastern coast is almost a continuous wall of high cliffs, whereas on the western coast there are shoals running miles out into the sea. Tamsui, Keelung, Anping, and Takao are known as open ports, and there are other minor ports for Chinese junks. With the exception of Keelung and Takao, they are little better than open roadsteads. Even the former two were not commodious enough, and were far from affording safe shelter in the monsoon and typhoon season. No trace can be found of the Chinese ever having made any attempt at improving the accommodation of these ports.

The Japanese Government saw that harbour improvement was of positive importance to the island from the point of view of communications and commerce. Consequently harbour construction was started on an extensive scale, both at Keelung and Takao. Below is given a summary of the works in progress at these two sea-gates.

Keelung

Keelung is a thriving port at the northern extremity of the island, containing a population of over fifty thousand souls. In the early days of the Japanese occupation, the harbour basin was very shallow, and its waters ran high for a full half of the year owing to the strong monsoon, so that vessels of 1,000 tons or more had to drop anchor about one mile off-shore.

Beginning in 1896, a series of investigations and surveys were conducted, resulting in the adoption of a plan for the improvement of the harbour. The work was taken in hand in 1899 as a four year's continuous undertaking at an estimated cost of 2,440,000 yen. The work consisted in dredging the basin, reclaiming shoals and constructing a provisional pier. The engineering work was meant to meet the most immediate needs only. Since then harbour extension programmes have at several times been adopted. The whole harbour improvement work, extending over quite twenty-eight years, at an estimated cost of over 22,068,946 yen, is expected to be completed in 1926. The work when completed, will give the port of Keelung the striking facilities which follow:

1. Eleven vessels ranging from 5,000 to 10,000 tons can be moored alongside the newly built embankment, and four alongside the old one, while six can be anchored at the buoys.
2. A portion measuring 397 *ken* of the new embankment will be appropriated to the exclusive purpose of shipping coal, which is expected to amount to 800,000 tons a year. And along the embankment, a goodly number of sheds, warehouses, godowns, and cranes will be erected.
3. Two docks will be constructed with capacity to accommodate 3,000 ton and 10,000 ton ships, respectively.

The harbour improvements up to the end of the fiscal year 1921–1922 are as follows:

1. Anchorage area. In the outer harbour, 340,600 *tsubo* with a depth of over 30 feet; in inner harbour 205,619 *tsubo* with a depth of 24 to 32 feet.
2. In the outer anchorage are there are two mooring buoys and in the inner harbour there are ten mooring buoys, and three floating piers

made of steel concrete. Four navigation buoys are set up as passage marks between the outer and the inner harbour.

3. Two break-waters, 180 *ken* long; the embankment wall 1127 *ken* in length. A railway extended out to the embankment. Sheds and warehouses equipped with several cranes of modern type. A concrete pavement 430 *ken* long. Bridge, canals and other requisite facilities for shipping are completed.

Takao

Takao is an important port in the south as Keelung is in the north, and is located on a narrow bay or lagoon. This lake-shaped bay extends sixteen miles in length from the north-west to the south-east, and is separated from the sea by a long stretch of sand-bank. A water-way, only 350 feet wide, forms its entrance, connecting the basins with the open sea. The lagoon was originally extremely shallow, and the entrance was strewn with sunken rocks so that even junks and small steamers found it difficult of approach.

Such being the case, the need of improving the port was forcibly brought home to the authorities. As steps preliminary to regular harbour construction, the reclamation of the foreshore and the dredging of the harbour basin were undertaken, and completed four years later. These works afforded the port considerable shipping facilities. Subsequently, on the conclusion of the Russo-Japan war, a general business boom reached the island; and this, coupled with the remarkable development of interest in the southern region, created heavy demands upon the limited capacity of the port of Takao. In view of this, the Government secured a vote of 4,733,000 yen in 1907, and 12,784,000 yen in 1912 from the Imperial Diet for the purpose of improving Takao harbour. With this appropriation, a huge-scale undertaking covering eighteen years in execution (1908–1925) was taken in hand. The work is now making good headway.

An outline sketch of the plan is as follows:

1. To provide accommodation for vessels of 10,000 tons to moor alongside the embankment; to establish facilities for connecting the land and water traffic, and to provide transport facilities for goods amounting to 900,000 tons a year.
2. To channel a navigation route from the open sea to the entrance, to construct from the south side a breakwater over 2280 feet long and to form from north to south a wall extending 760 feet to protect the harbour from sand and breakers.
3. To widen the entrance to a width of 500 feet and to extend the water area inside the harbour to 544,000 *tsubo* with a depth at low tide of 30 feet; to place in position navigation and mooring buoys, and to construct an embankment 730 *ken* long and other necessary shore equipment.

The harbour construction so far as it has progressed is as follows:

1. The breakwater 2,189 feet long has been constructed. Mud and Sand to the extent of 2,560,000 cubic *tsubo* have been dredged. A water area covering 274,520 *tsubo* with a depth, at low tide, of 18 to 30 feet has been constituted inside the harbour; and a water area of 61,600 *tsubo* has been constituted on the navigation route outside.

2. The rocks at the entrance have been removed, two navigation signals outside the harbour and twelve mooring buoys placed in position. An embankment to a length of 480 *ken* completed. The other necessary buildings, numerous cranes, roads, canals, light-draught steamers, etc., are already in existence. Six steamers of more than 8,000 tons can be moored at the embankment and at the mooring buoys, 12 altogether.

River Improvement

As stated in the first chapter, the rivers of Taiwan, taking as they do their sources in the central high mountains, have their upper streams rushing and torrential. But as they flow down to the level country, they get split up into many small irregular streams or are almost lost in large river beds. On the occurrence of typhoons and during the period of rainfalls, these quiet rivers rise to an enormous extent, and become roaring and wild torrents, causing a clamant danger to traffic and to cultivated fields.

These conditions may be attributed in large measure to the neglect of river system improvement.

The need for riparian works was long keenly felt, but they were delayed owing to financial limitations and the prior claims of other undertakings of a more urgent nature. It was in 1912 that the River Improvement Investigation Commission was formed; and the Commission started the work of surveying nine principal rivers for a period of five consecutive years, at an estimated expenditure of 100,000 yen a year. As a result of these investigations, concrete plans for the improvement and maintenance of the principal river systems, and for water utilization, were determined on and put into execution.

The works have by this time made notable progress,

so that security has been ensured in many places for the fields and dwellings bordering on the rivers, and vast tracts of waste land and river beds are being brought under cultivation.

9

Productive Industries

Agriculture

SITUATED between the tropical and sub-tropical zones, the island is endowed with a variety of favourable natural conditions. The climate and soil are remarkably fit for agriculture. It is stated on good authority that the Chinese Government considered Formosa a great granary, and that the Chinese immigrants themselves clearly designed to make the island an agricultural colony. When the Japanese commenced the colonization of the island, they first of all attached great importance to the development of agriculture. The measures adopted for such purposes by the industrial administration have resulted in increasing the quantity and in raising the quality, of agricultural products.

According to the statistical returns, the total agricultural production in 1923 amounted to 192,939,416 yen in value, which shows a striking increase as compared with 101,233,509 in 1913.

The agricultural output more than meets domestic needs, and the entire surplus is exported to Japan proper and many foreign countries. Investigations made in 1923 show that the arable land then covered an area of 775,400 *ko* as against 363,290 *ko* surveyed in 1899. According to official reports, at the end of 1923, there were found 2,262,891 people engaged in agricultural industries, that is, more than 58 percent of the total population of the island. The principal agricultural products of the island, given in the order of relative importance, comprise rice, sugar, tea, sweet potatoes, peanut, peas and beans, sesame, barley and wheat, ramie, jute, indigo and tree-indigo, tobacco, aurantia, bananas, pineapples, longan fruits, and vegetables.

Formosan Farmers Pumping Water

Principal products

Rice

The soil and climate of the island are eminently suited to the cultivation of rice; this is especially the case in the western districts, where crops are raised twice a year.

The Japanese authorities have spared no effort to

improve the quality and yield of rice by recommending a scientific system of irrigating and fertilizing the soil and also by the standardization of seed.

Today the rice-growing industry has undergone decided developments in all directions. Specialists on rice cultivation speak of the possibility of obtaining three crops instead of two a year in many districts. This total output of rice in 1923 reached 4,866,087 *koku*, valued at 85,680,000 yen.

Sugar

The cultivation of sugar cane appears to have followed closely upon the settlement of the Chinese in South Formosa. When Dutch adventurers occupied the island in 1624, they found sugar one of the principal articles of export. Under Koxinga's régime and in subsequent periods the production of sugar was warmly encouraged, the colonists being taught new methods of its cultivation and manufacture. Owing to the somewhat arbitrary and unsuitable system adopted by the Chinese authorities, however, not so much progress had been effected in the industry as should have been made.

At the time Taiwan came under Japanese rule, the industry was in a sorely neglected condition, the annual production of sugar amounting only to some 90,000,000 *kin*.

In those days, the annual consumption of sugar in Japan proper was more than 500,000,000 *kin*, so that the output of her new colony could scarcely meet one-fourth of her requirements. The Japanese immediately saw that Taiwan, possessing unique advantages for cane cultivation, was evidently destined to play an important part in the sugar trade, and that government assistance in building up this industry would be most fruitful in results. Accordingly the Government engaged Dr. Nitobe, Ph.D., a well-known economist and scholar, to make investigations into the future prospects of the sugar industry in the island. Dr. Nitobe submitted a very interesting report on the subject, making strong recommendations on the following points: introduction of superior varieties of canes, improved cultivation and fertilization, better irrigation, improvements in crushing machinery and methods of manufacture, opening up new land for cane cultivation and the replacement of rice-fields by cane plantations. He was personally confident that the production could be increased fivefold within ten years.

All his recommendations were received with much favour. In consequence, a Special Sugar Bureau was established in 1902 and at the same time the Sugar Industry Encouragement Ordinance was promulgated. The Government granted subsidies totalling 12,238,734 yen up to 1921 as a positive encouragement of this industry. With the view of obtaining the varieties of cane best suited to the climate, the Government imported various cane cuttings and seedlings from Java, Hawaii, Cuba, Louisiana and Australia.

Lahaina and *Rose Bamboo*, which were varieties obtained from Hawaii gave excellent results, and were found to yield a harvest two or three times as great as the indigenous varieties. Accordingly the Government largely distributed seedlings of them among cane planters. In later years, the Government made a free distribution of Java superior seedlings and Taiwan superior ones. Thus the Government concentrated great efforts upon the improvement of existing canes and the introduction of superior varieties.

In the sugar manufacturing season 1902–1902 [sic], sugar plantations covered an area of 118,888 *ko* producing cane amounting to 4,938,300,000 *kin* as compared with the cane area of 116,620 *ko* yielding a crop of 6,631,863,843 *kin* in the season of 1922–1923.

These figures sufficiently indicate what a tremendous development has taken place in the sugar industry of Taiwan during the past ten years.

Tea

In the list of Taiwan industries, tea forms an important article of trade; and it justifies a brief description.

According to the latest statistics, the total production of Taiwan tea stood at 20,000,000 *kin*, of which about 9,000,000 yen worth was exported.

It cannot be definitely ascertained whether tea plants were found growing wild in this island, or whether they were introduced from China.

The cultivation and manufacture of tea, however, undoubtedly dates subsequently to the Chinese emigration to the island. It was completely unknown to the aborigines.

Up to 1854, Taiwan tea was shipped to Amoy, where it was refined and transshipped for the United States. But from 1868 onwards, tea was prepared in this island for shipment direct to foreign countries, by skilled tea men brought over from Amoy and Foochow.

Robert Swinhoe, British Consul at Tamsui, may be called the discoverer of the Taiwan tea industry and John Dodd the promoter. John Dodd, who established himself in the tea business in the island in 1869, made a trial shipment of tea direct to New York. From an export of 210,000 *kin*, the trade increased to 1,000,000 km in 1870 and prices rose from $15 to $30 per 100 *kin*. Thus the Taiwan tea trade went on assuming notable proportions, but in 1883 it experienced a considerable depression.

Chinese speculators now stepped in and shipped the congested stock of Oolong tea to Foochow, where it was re-manufactured into Pouchong tea or scented tea. Later, the manufacture of Pouchong tea was started in the island.

The Plantation and Tea Picking Girls

On arrival in Taiwan, the Japanese authorities appreciated what the future of the tea industry had in store and at the same time they noticed with regret that so much inferior Chinese tea was being imported and mixed up with genuine Taiwan tea and exported as pure Taiwan tea. In August, 1898, the Government issued an order, instructing the individuals engaged in the preparation and sale of tea, to form a Tea Merchants Guild, with the object of preventing the manufacture and sale of adulterated teas and of sustaining the high character of Taiwan tea.

The Japanese also saw that the existing organization of the tea trade was in so primitive and complicated a condition that the tea had, after it was picked, to pass through far too many middle men before reaching the American and European markets. This leaves even yet much room for immediate improvement. The Government authorities are encouraging the establishment of tea manufacturing companies or incorporations with a view to increasing the production of machine-made tea by supplying them with the necessary machinery and implements for the manufacture of tea. Before the tea industry came under the supervision of the government, the tea planters used no fertilizers of any kind on account of misconceptions entertained by them, with the result that the quality of their tea was becoming deteriorated.

In view of this fact, the Government in 1909 commenced the free distribution of bean cake among the tea growers for the purpose of fertilizers and the free distribution of tea seedlings.

The Government authorities are now devoting special attention to the development of tea plantations, the increase of tea production, and the improvement of the quality of tea. It is anticipated with good reason that before long a marked progress will be witnessed in the tea industry of Taiwan.

The Taiwan teas are mainly represented by Oolong tea and Pouchong tea, but green and black teas are also produced. The green tea is mostly supplied to local consumers; the black tea is extending its market in Japan and abroad on account of its superior quality. As by-products of these different teas, powdered tea, coarse tea and stem-tea may be mentioned. Powdered tea is used as raw material for making caffeine; this new-born industry has a promising future. Coarse and stem-teas are exported to Singapore, South China, and the Luchow Islands.

Oolong tea is the pure leaf, free from the addition of any colouring or flavouring matter. Compared with Chinese teas, it is subjected to a minimum of manipulation, and the process of preparation is comparatively simple. The aromatic and pungent flavour of Oolong tea is highly appreciated in America; in England the importation is almost exclusively used for blending with other teas to give flavour to the latter.

With the advent of the tea picking season, the Daitotei

market and the country present a lively and picturesque scene. In Daitotei, crowds of young women dressed in their best, and coquettishly adorned with strongly scented blossoms, overrun the place from morning to night. In the tea grounds, groups of young maidens attractively dressed in bright colours are found picking tea leaves, laughing and chatting together, with markets strapped on their backs. These Taiwan damsels look upon the tea picking period as the opening of the social season, as it were, and their fortune is envied by their more aristocratic sisters who are apt to suffer from ennui in their secluded chambers.

Formosan Girls Sorting Tea

Sweet Potato

The sweet potato is an indispensable article of diet, next in importance to rice. The warm climate of the island, with very rare visitations of frost, is well adapted for its growth. This plant is cultivated almost all over the island throughout all seasons. The crop is mostly consumed in the island, some portion of it being exported to China in dried scraps and as material for making spirit. The production of sweet potato in 1923 amounted to more than 1,643,853,068 *kin*. The output of the rest of the agricultural products in 1923 is shown below.

Category	Crop
Peanuts	350,250 *koku*
Beans	92,209 *koku*
Wheat and Barley	21,589 *koku*
Sesame Seed	12,789 *koku*
Jute	5,537,443 *kin*
Ramie	1,864,922 *kin*
Indigo	2,591,499 *kin*
Tobacco	1739,545 *kin*
Aurantia	22,545,668 *kin*
Banana	188,778,634 *kin*
Pine-apples	1,924,765 *piece*
Lychees	28,813,758 *kin*

Stock farming

The cattle of the island chiefly consist of water buffaloes, zebus, foreign and cross-bred cattle. The water-buffaloes, which are found in vast numbers, are large and strong but of quiet disposition. Their universal drawback is that they require to be sprinkled with water several times while engaged at work.

The zebu is small and not so strong, but he has the advantage of being more agile and requires no bathing. The cattle are mostly employed for draught and agricultural purposes. Foreign and cross-bred cattle are raised only for milking. Of late, Indian cattle have been imported for the purpose of improving the indigenous zebus or yellow ox. The total number of all these cattle in 1897 was 192,825; and this number increased in a remarkable fashion to 491,305 in 1923. This number includes 391,751 head of buffaloes, 96,136 head of zebus and 3,418 head of western Indian and cross-bred cattle.

The rearing of swine is an important domestic industry among the Formosans. As pork forms one of the most prized daily articles of popular food, its consumption is steadily increasing. During the year 1923 the number of swine reared reached the considerable total of 1,317,106. The number of poultry bred totalled 5,176,214.

The Government have for years past made considerable efforts towards the improvement of live-stock by introducing occidental cattle and swine and Indian cows.

In former times, rinderpest, swine-cholera, and other live-stock epidemics ravaged the island in a dreadful manner, causing severe losses to the farmers. But these horrible animal diseases have now practically disappeared, owing to the rigorous scientific measures taken by the Government authorities.

Manufacturing Industry

With the exception of the sugar and tea industries, the Manufacturing industries of the island have not yet assumed such proportions as to be of importance to the trade of the world. As Taiwan is essentially an agricultural country, considerable progress has been made in the manufacture of agricultural products.

Saké-brewing, the manufacture of materials for public works and buildings, as also household industries, have attained a stage of notable development.

The many new industries such as the manufacture of machinery and various chemical industries which sprung up rapidly as an outcome of the great boom created by the World war are now undergoing a severe ordeal in the shape of the post-bellum economic depression now sweeping over the world. The total value of the goods turned out from these industrial factories during 1923 amounted to 205,841,679 yen.

The following is a general classification of the various industries.

1. The preparation and manufacture of agricultural products includes the sugar industry, rice-unhulling and rice-cleaning, the tea industry, flour-milling, pine-apple canning and so forth.
2. Among sake-brewing industries, the manufacture of beer, Japanese saké, and Chinese liquors may be mentioned.
3. In the manufacture of materials for public works and building, there are equipped factories for making cement, brick, slate, marble and lime.
4. The household industries comprise the manufacture of hats, wood-work, mats, shell-flower work, vermicelli, shoes, pith-paper, incense-sticks, candles, artificial flowers, silver and gold articles etc.
5. The iron-works which were established, as a result of the war boom, at Keelung, Taihoku and Takao have greatly extended their plans and are now capable of manufacturing ships, sugar-manufacturing machinery, large-sized boilers, steam-engines, and other machinery.
6. In the field of chemical industries, several factories have been established for the manufacture of sulphuric acid, superphosphate, fertilizer, soda-ash, soap, and carbide.

They are making successful efforts to do business. Among the spinning industries, not to mention jute spinning, which has succeeded well, the China grass and cotton spinning industries are regarded as having a promising future.

Of the various industries dealt with above, those that have the most important bearing upon foreign trade are the sugar and tea industries. According to the business results during the season of 1922–1923, the total capital invested in the sugar industry amount amounted to 27,000,000 yen, the modern equipped factories in operation numbered 44, the aggregate pressing capacity for 24 hours was 34,650 tons. The total production of sugar was 581,000,000 *kin*, and the value of sugar exported to Japan proper and abroad amounted to upwards of 114,000,000 yen.

Mining Industry

Taiwan abounds in valuable mineral resources. The minerals licenses to work which have been granted are thirteen in number, viz. gold, gold and copper ore, gold and silver ore, gold dust, copper, cupreous iron sulphide, quicksilver, iron sand, coal, brown coal, petroleum, sulphur, and phosphorite.

The aggregate mineral production for the year 1923 amounted in value to 12,910,000 yen. With the exception of the working of gold, copper and coal, the exploitation of mines in the island is in an undeveloped stage, but has nevertheless a great future before it. The authorities are taking all measures available to give material encouragement to mining operations.

They publish in print the results of mining investigations, geological surveys, prospecting for useful minerals, and mineralogical and metallurgical researches, carried out by them. Further, free distribution is made among interested individuals and companies, of annual reports containing many statistics and describing concessions.

Of these minerals, the following, viz.: – coal, gold, copper, petroleum and sulphur, are produced in considerable quantities and are worth special mention.

Coal

Coal deposits are found in the northern, central and southern parts of the island, but the only seams which appear likely to prove profitable are found in the northern districts, where 90 per cent of the whole output is produced. The coal veins always run double, and are from forty to fifty feet apart. The coal mining industry dates as far back as the year 1642, when the Dutch occupied Keelung and Tamsui. It was, however, checked for a long period of years on account of the superstition of the islanders. In 1870, official permission was given for the operation of coal mines throughout the island.

Since Taiwan came under Japanese rule, coal mining operations have been encouraged by the granting of many concessions, and modern mining machinery has been installed in many mines. Owing to the rapid development of various industries, there arose an increased demand for coal. Remarkable progress has thus been effected in this industry during recent years. The output in 1923 was nearly 1,440,000 tons, amounting in value to 1,141,000 yen, indicating bright prospects for the future of the industry.

Gold

The gold mining industry comes next in importance. According to the mineralogical survey so far as carried out, gold is found existing in the extreme north. This industry comprises two lines, dust and ore.

The placer mining dates as far back as three hundred years ago. It was about thirty years ago that a discovery was made of gold layers in the north. Subsequently the amount of gold production has yearly increased in a truly remarkable fashion. The most noted gold mines are those of Zuiho and Kinkwaser, where operations are actively going on. The total yield of gold during 1923 amounted to 1,119,980 *momme* valued at 556,000 yen.

Copper and copper ore

The mining of copper may be traced back to the discovery of the mineral amidst gold deposits, which was made in 1905. The copper obtained was of excellent quality, and its production has since steadily increased year by year. The total output of the mineral in 1923 amounted to the value of 54,966 yen, and of copper ore, to the value of 4,900 yen.

Petroleum

According to the old records, the credit of having first called attention to the Formosan petroleum deposits belongs to John Dodd. In 1860, he commenced collecting oil on the savage border (Shinchiku districts) in cooperation with some Chinese. He was, however, obliged to abandon his plans owing to the interference of the Chinese mandarins. Twelve years later, the Chinese engaged two American experts and started boring operations. Not long after this, the American experts, dissatisfied with the treatment meted out to them, left the island, and the work was discontinued.

No attempt had since been made to work the oil fields until the Japanese interested themselves in oil developments. In 1904, a tentative excavation was carried out by the Oil Men's Corporation of Taiwan, and met with good success. The industry was subsequently transferred to the management of the Hoden Petroleum Company and since November 1921, it has been placed under the control of the Nippon Petroleum Company.

Prior to the Japanese occupation, there was only one known oil-field. The scientific surveying strenuously conducted for years by the Japanese Government disclosed that quite a surprising number of petroleum veins exist throughout the island. In view of the large returns brought by the developed oil fields of the world, it is of interest to note that Taiwan offers a sphere with a promising future for this industry. The production of petroleum for 1923 was approximately 14,000 *koku* amounting in value to 186,000 yen.

Sulphur

Though some deposits of this mineral are found in other districts, Taihoku Province contains the principal solfataras. The extreme northern district, covered by the Daiton range of volcanic mountains, the highest peak of which attains an altitude of over 3,600 feet, abounds in sulphur pits. It is reported that while the island was in Spanish occupation, sulphur was obtained from these mountain crevices. During the days of the Dutch and Koxinga, scanty attention was seemingly given to the sulphur deposits of the island. After the establishment of the Chinese Government, however, sulphur became a source of careful inquiry. Liu Ming-chuan, a Chinese governor of progressive spirit, took up the industry as government business and set up a Sulphur Bureau.

During the early days of the Japanese occupation, there was much fluctuation in the amount of sulphur produced, owing to the effect of dull markets abroad. Subsequently, however, there occurred an increased demand for sulphur, when the average annual output amounted to 5,000,000 *kin*. In 1923, the production was reduced to 1,880,000 *kin* representing a value of 43,000 yen.

Forestry

Well-nigh one half of the surface of the island being covered with high mountains rising to a height of 6,000–9,000 feet to 12,000–13,000 feet above sea-level, there exists a large area of magnificent primeval forest.

The forests bordering on the plain had, under the Chinese régime, been to a great extent denuded of trees, owing partly to reclamation for agricultural purposes, and partly to fires and indiscriminate felling for timber and fuel, without any attempt at re-afforestation. The re-afforestation work was taken in hand after the advent of the Japanese, but has not yet made any notable progress. Accordingly the unexploited primeval forests are now only to be found in the rugged high mountains far beyond the access of civilized settlers. The forests of Taiwan, owing to their geographical position, geological qualities, and climatic conditions, comprise an amazingly large variety of trees belonging to the tropical, sub-tropical, temperate and even the semi-arctic, zones. It is no wonder that the Portuguese navigators looking up at the green verdant mountains from the high exclaimed: "Isle of Beauty!"

Among many large forests so far discovered, the most renowned are the Arisan, Hassenzan and Dakusui-kei forests, where exploitation is being actively carried on under the Government Forestry Bureau. In 1923, the volume of timber disposed of by the Government amounted to over 298,990 *koku*, representing 3,559,000 yen in value. Of the three great forests, the Arisan forest is the most

Sacred Tree at Mt. Arisan

important, standing foremost in respect of extent, wealth and beauty, and is fast becoming known to Japanese and Westerners as well. Arisan is the name given to a range of mountains stretching westward from Mt. Niitaka, and is situated about forty miles east of Kagi. The forest lies at an altitude ranging from 2,800 feet to 8,700 feet above sea level, covering an area of 11,000 *chobu* (27,000 acres). The timber obtainable from the forest is estimated at 22,000,000 board feet. As for the distribution of the predominant trees, *benihi* (*Chamaecyparis formosensis*) grows mingled with other trees at an altitude of 6,000 feet above sea level, and from 7,000 feet upwards are founds in turn woods, all composed of *benihi* and *hinoki* (*Chantaecyparis obtusa*), while *tsuge* (*tsuge formosa*) and *himekomalsn* (*pinus parviflora*) are found mingled together at 8,000 feet. These innumerable trees form the magnificent primeval forests that have remained sacred and untouched from time immemorial.

The exploitation of the Arisan forests was started as a private undertaking by Fujita & Co., but was transferred to the Government through purchase in 1910. A railway more than 54 miles in length has been constructed for the transport of timber from the forests. The railway section from Kogi to Takezaki is opened to general traffic, but the line beyond Takezaki is very steep and is not open for public use.

Special permission will, however, be given to visitors to Mt. Arisan to avail themselves of the line. The forest railway steams up, crawling along rugged mountains and sharp cliffs in a spiral fashion, and reaches the high elevation of 8,000 feet. The train in its journey passes through more than 73 tunnels as well innumerable cuttings. The grand kaleidoscopic views and exciting experiences one can enjoy while ascending lofty mountains and traversing deep valleys are simply wonderful and quite beyond description.

By means of aerial cables, the timber felled is conveyed and gathered at points accessible to railway stations, and then transported down to the Saw Mills and Kagi, a distance of forty miles. The volume of timber obtained during 1923 amounted to 190,332 *koku* corresponding to the value of 2,447,592 yen.

The lumbering business figures show that the Arisan forests alone are capable of yielding more than half of the whole production of the island and this vouches for a further development of the lumber industry in the same forests.

These primeval forests contain large numbers of old trees which have passed beyond their mature stage. The Government, therefore, has formed the plan of renovating the Arisan forests by felling aged trees and reafforesting them afterwards. The Government is also carrying out afforestation schemes in various districts, and is giving encouragement to private parties to engage in the same useful work. During 1923 the extent of newly planted land afforested both by the government and by private parties amounted to approximately 121,777 *chobu*.

Marine Industry

As Formosa extends over the tropics and the temperate zone, the finny tribes are found in great abundance throughout all seasons in the waters around. Great catches can be made in the seas off the northern and southwestern parts of the island and also around the Pescadores. In the year 1910 when the Government brought the fishing industry under its direct control, catches amounted only to 960,000 yen in value as compared with the piscicultural output in 1923, amounting in value to 9,003,651 yen.

According to the special census taken in 1905, only 2.4 per cent of the island population were engaged in fishery and the salt-making industry. These figures sufficiently show how the marine industry had been neglected. Since the Government has taken an active interest in the industry, special efforts have been made in the matter of conducting studies and experiments with a view to developing the industry. Among the many measures taken for its promotion, the establishment of a Fisheries Section of the Department of Productive Industries, the purchase of experimental fishing boats and the constitution of a piscicultural section and a marine observation board are worth mentioning.

As shown below, the value of aquatic products and their preparations for 1923 shows a remarkable increase over the figures for 1908.

	1908	1923
Total aquatic output	7,785,643 yen	14,273,730 yen
Fish Catches	4,044,334 yen	9,030,851 yen
Marine manufactures	1,553,969 yen	3,299,514 yen
Pisciculture	2,167,340 yen	1,943,355 yen

Fishery

The fishing industry of the island is now on the high road to extensive development. The work is most actively carried on with good returns, at Keelung and Takao in Chinese fishing craft and petroleum motor boats. The principal catches include bonito, sea-bream, tunny, shark, spear-fish and so on. Above all, red-sea-breams, or *Akadai* as the fish is commonly known, are caught in such great quantities as to form a leading article of diet among the people. Owing to a rapid increase of fish catches during the winter in recent years, considerable quantities of fresh fish are exported to Japan proper.

Marine manufactures

Among the manufactures of marine products, dried bonito, sodabushi, boiled and dried sardines, shark fins and karasumi – caviare made from grey mullet – are the principal. The bulk of these preparations being intended for the use of the Formosans, the manufacturing methods are not carried on in modern fashion. The climatic conditions are not ideal for the manufacture of dried salt fish. Yet as there is a growing demand for this foodstuff in the island and in China, the industry has a promising future. Though the manufacture of dried bonito was started scarcely a dozen years ago, it has developed in proportion with the progress of bonito catching. The production during 1923 amounted to the value of 2,109,546 yen.

Fish breeding

Fish culture is a time-honoured industry. Twenty years ago, the production from this source far exceeded that derived from sea-catches. There are two kinds of fish-breeding ponds, one with salt water and the other with fresh water, covering an area of 24,306 *ko*. Oysters, lobsters, milk-fish and mullets are raised in salt water ponds. In fresh water ponds are reared several kinds of fish, many of which (with the exception of a carp), are introduced from the main land.

10

Trade and Finance

TRADE with foreign countries is carried on through the four open ports, viz., Keelung, Tamsui, Anping and Takao. Besides, there are several minor ports specially opened for facilitating Chinese junk trade. Keelung and Takao are the two most important and thriving ports. As harbour improvements are in progress, the future of trade and shipping at these two ports is assured. The trade of Formosa has made remarkable strides since it became a Japanese possession. The total volume of exports and imports for the year 1897 amounted scarcely to 31,000,000 yen. This figure swelled to over 380,000,000 yen in 1923, showing the enormous increase of one thousand per cent within a space of twenty-five years. Seventy to eighty per cent of the trade was with Japan proper. For instance, the total value of trade with foreign countries amounted to only 68,200,000 yen in 1923 whereas the trade with Japan proper reached the level of 240,460,000 yen in value. In the same year the total value of exports amounted to about 198,590,000 yen, the total value of imports reaching approximately 110,120,000 yen, recording an excess of exports to the amount of over 88,460,000 yen.

The following table shows the import and export trade with foreign countries and Japan proper during 1923.

Total value of trade	308,724,294 yen
Exports to foreign countries	29,152,437 yen
Imports from foreign countries	39,111,367 yen
Total foreign trade	68,263,804 yen
Aggregate exports	198,594,802 yen
Aggregate imports	110,124,492 yen
Favourable balance of trade	88,466,310 yen

Finance

The finance of the Formosan Government is managed under the Special Account, so named in distinction from the General Budget of the Empire, which was instituted in the year 1897. Since Formosa came under Japanese rule, the expenditure of the island was met partly from the revenue of the island, partly by a subsidy from the Imperial Government Treasury. According to the original arrangement, it was expected that until 1910 Formosa would continue to be a drain upon the Home Treasury. The annual income of the island, however, increased by leaps and bounds with each year so that Formosa became independent of Treasury aid in 1905; that is, five years earlier than was previously anticipated. Moreover, a portion of the customs duties and the whole amount of the sugar consumption-tax were subsequently credited to the general account of Japan proper. This fact sufficiently testifies to the substantial foundation secured for the island finance.

In the fiscal year 1893, the revenue of Formosa stood at 11,282,265 yen as against an expenditure of 10,487,610 yen.

Since then the annual revenue has continuously increased until in 1923 it rose to the record breaking figure of over 110,000,000 yen. In 1922, owing to the world-wide business depression, the Government revenue notably diminished. Nevertheless a budget of 106,002,030 yen was prepared. It may be added that the estimate of revenue for the fiscal year 1924–1925 is 91,594,033 yen.

11

Government Monopolies

THE Government of Formosa possesses five monopolies, viz., opium, camphor, salt, tobacco and alcoholic liquors. These were organized in the following years respectively.

- Opium, 1896
- Camphor, 1899
- Salt, 1899
- Tobacco, 1905
- Liquors, 1922

Opium

When Formosa passed into Japanese hands, one of the most important and urgent problems that confronted the Government authorities was how to deal with the ruinous habit of opium smoking from which the inhabitants had long suffered. Under the then existing circumstances it was believed that the success of our administration in the island depended upon the ability of our authorities to solve this great problem.

After mature consideration, the authorities determined

that to attempt to abolish the evil practice all at once would be an unwise and dangerous policy. So they decided to adopt a measure of gradual suppression based upon the principal of strict eventual prohibition.

Consequently, in January 1897, the Opium Control Regulations were issued which prohibited the importation, cultivation and manufacture of opium, and restricted the smoking of the substance, special licenses being granted to confirmed smokers to use government opium for medicinal purposes. As had been expected, this gradual suppression scheme has achieved remarkable success, as is testified by the heavy decrease in the number of opium users and in the quantity of opium paste sold. During the past few years, however, much fluctuation has not been noticed in the total value of opium paste sold. This is due first to the fact that the smokers have shown a preference for superior opium over inferior stuff, and secondly to the fact that for many reasons the selling prices have frequently been raised. But there are now indications pointing to a gradual decrease in the volume of sales of opium paste in future years. At the time the opium monopoly was introduced, there were 170,000 opium smokers, the present number is 40,000 and in the course of twenty years we expect there will be none.

Camphor Monopoly

Taiwan, widely known as the "Land of Camphor" yields the major proportion of the world's production. In 1899, the Taiwan government declared camphor a government monopoly, with the twofold object of improving the quality of the material and of securing a firm control of its output. On account of the well-standardized qualities of the stuff and of its moderate prices, the camphor of Taiwan has now taken a highly important place in the world market.

Camphor Still

Modern civilized life in Europe and America requires increasing quantities of camphor. The substance enters largely into the manufacture of celluloid. It is consumed in the preparation of medicinal drugs, perfume, disinfectants, and gun-powder, and it is used in religious services in India.

The prices of B-quality camphor for domestic use is ¥142 per 100 *kin* and improved B-quality ¥170 per 100 *kin*. The price of improved B-quality for foreign export is ¥163 for a piece 84 *kin* in weight.

Now that camphor plays so important a part as it does in the manufacture of celluloid, the demand is remarkably on the increase throughout Japan and the world.

When camphor chips go through the process of distillation, three kinds of camphor oil, white, red, and blue, are obtained. The first kind is commonly used in manufacturing industries as a substitute for turpentine oil and is used for deodorizing and insecticidal purposes. The second is chiefly used as material for making safrol, and the remnant is mixed with other substances for the above-mentioned purposes. The third is, to say nothing of its ordinary uses, employed for ore-separating purposes.

The annual production of camphor is subjected to variations, as the output of the material is so regulated as to meet the demand of the world market. According to the figures available, the annual production ranges from 5,000,000 *kin* to 6,000,000 *kin*. The quantity of camphor shipped during the fiscal year 1924 was 4,808,800 *kin*, the value of which including that of by-products, amounted to ¥1,107,000.

Salt

The Dutch, who were the first foreigners to occupy Formosa, did not allow any salt to be manufactured in the island, but imported the article from abroad through the Dutch East India Company. On the other hand, Koxinga who wished the island to become self-supporting, introduced the method of obtaining salt from seawater by the heat of the sun. When Formosa came into Chinese possession, salt was taxed and was subsequently turned into a monopoly industry. On the arrival of the Japanese in the island, the monopoly system was abolished and private individuals were allowed to manufacture and sell salt on their own account. This policy was adopted in the hope of benefiting the islanders but the results were disappointing. The salt pans were left to go to ruin with the consequent result of degeneration of the product and the price of salt rose remarkably. These conditions led to a large increase in the imports of salt from abroad. Such being the case, the Japanese Government decided to take the salt manufacture into their hands in 1899, with a view to resuscitating the declining business and ensuring the supply of a necessity of life for the islanders. The improvement measures had a remarkable effect in restoring and extending the salt pans, increasing the production of salt and stabilising its price. In short, the essence of the new policy adopted was not to increase the Government profit at the expense of the people but simply to balance revenue against expenditure.

Salt-Pans

Since the salt monopoly was put in force the salt area and salt production have steadily increased, so that this has now developed into a promising export commodity, finding its way to Japan proper, Korea, Karafuto, the littoral provinces of Eastern Russia, Manila and Hongkong, besides satisfying the needs of the islanders.

At the end of the year 1923, it was found that the salt pans covered 2,348 *ko*, yielding quantities amounting to over 389,670,000 *kin*. The collection of salt from the manufacturers is carried out through seven monopoly branch offices. In fixing the purchase prices, the economic conditions of the salt manufacturers and the amount of trouble entailed in manufacture are taken into consideration. The salt collected is classified into three grades, viz., refined, first and second, each of which is supplied to consumers at fixed rates; but if required for industrial encouragement purposes a special discount is allowed. According to the latest figures, more than 300,000,000 pounds of solar salt was obtained from the western sea coast, out of which 80,000,000 pounds was consumed in the island and 220,000,000 pounds shipped to Japan proper and abroad.

Tobacco

As Taiwan is situated in a unique region where nature means to have her way completely, the island possesses a soil and climatic conditions highly favourable to the growth of plant life. It is no wonder that in such circumstances there are found here quite a large variety of plants of economic value. None has a brighter future than tobacco, as there is a growing demand for the leaf not only in the island but also in the market abroad. According to experiments made as to the possibilities inherent in the cultivation of various economic plants, tobacco appears to give the best results. Before the Japanese came to the island, tobacco planting had not been much attended to, as the production of tea and camphor had been found more profitable. In those days, Taiwan used to obtain most of her tobacco from the mainland. In many districts, the savage tribes grew enough of the plant for their own consumption and in some cases they produced a certain amount for barter with the Formosans.

Experts report that in some districts the plants generally thrive well, and the leaves are large and attractive, and that if the hill planters were taught the proper method of curing and preparing the leaf, the resulting product would be good quality.

It may be interesting to note that the savages prepare the leaf for smoking in many curious shapes, as, for instance, in the form of a club, a large radish, or that of a cheroot.

All the savages, men, women and children, are fond of tobacco smoking.

Following the example set by the Home Government in 1904, the Government of Taiwan introduced the tobacco monopoly system in the ensuing year, mainly with the object of securing a source of revenue. The result has been considerably successful, as there has occurred an increasing demand for the article, owing to the increase of wealth on the part of the islanders and to their advanced standard of living. The proceeds of tobacco sales during 1923 amounted in value to 11,000,000 yen.

The tobacco put on the market comprises three kinds, namely, Japan-made, foreign-made and Taiwan-made. The Taiwan-made tobacco originally consisted of cut tobacco only, made by private individuals; in 1912, the Monopoly Bureau commenced manufacturing cigars and cigarettes in addition to cut tobacco, making use of up-to-date electric motor machines. At present, light grades of cut tobacco, two grades of cigarettes with mouth pieces, six grades of cigarettes, and eight grades of cigars are turned out by the Monopoly Bureau. Among these different grades of tobacco, No. 2 and No. 3 Jasmine cigarettes, and Niitaka, Niitaka Extra and Tsugitaka cigars are considered to be of excellent quality and are favourably received by the discriminating public.

The leaf material required for cut tobacco manufacture was formerly imported from China, amounting in weight to about 4,000,000 *kin* annually. Considering that a keenly regrettable thing, the Government has endeavoured to improve the quality of the home-grown tobacco leaf. Successful results have been attained, so that at present the necessary supply of good tobacco leaf can be, and is, produced in the island. The yield for 1922 amounted to 2,720,000 *kin*. Besides, the experimental cultivation of American yellow leaves and other varieties considered good for the manufacture of cigars and cigarettes has been entered upon and has likewise given satisfactory results. It may be added that the tobacco leaves grown by the savage tribes amount to approximately 2,000,000 *kin* a year.

Alcoholic liquors

The alcoholic liquors that are consumed in Taiwan at present may be divided into three different groups in respect of the place of production, namely, those made in Taiwan, those imported from Japan proper and those imported from China and Western countries.

In respect of manufacturing methods, they may again be classified into three different kinds, viz., those brewed, those distilled and those which have been subjected to further process of working and preparation after having been brewed and distilled.

It was in 1907 that a tax was for the first time imposed upon alcoholic liquors. Since then, though there have been many changes in taxation rates and the method of tax collection, the receipts from the tax have been steadily on the increase. The saké tax collected in the earlier years hardly amounted to half a million yen, but, after a period of 15 years, this leapt up to over five million yen.

The Monopoly Act regarding alcoholic liquors was passed and put into operation in July 1922. There were two important reasons for the institution of the Liquor Monopoly. One reason was that the authorities found it necessary and advisable from the standpoint of public health and in order to improve the manufacture and quality of the liquors to place the liquor business under the immediate supervision of the Government. The other was the need of creating a new source of revenue to meet the ever-growing expenditure. Seeing that in western countries, hot discussions are being held upon the question of the control or prohibition of the use of alcoholic liquors from moral, religious and sanitary points of view, the monopoly system of the liquors adopted in Taiwan may be called a progressive and well-intended policy. The Government and the public in Taiwan have the responsibility of carrying out this this system to the best advantage.

The Government monopoly includes all kinds of alcoholic liquors (the brewing and sale of beer being temporarily excepted). Spirits intended exclusively for the requirements of the island are directly dealt in by the Government and those to be exported abroad are allowed to be manufactured by private parties. In case the Government considers it profitable to purchase liquors from Japan proper or from foreign countries, they secure the needed supply direct from the exporting countries or through their agents. The average consumption of alcoholic liquors per year amounts to upwards of 200,000 *koku*.

12

Social Work

THE social work now being carried on in the island may be divided into three kinds; first, charity and relief work; second, social reform work; third, protection and culture work. Though the latter two categories are comparatively of recent origin, yet the first category has been in practice since Chinese days.

While Taiwan was under the Chinese régime, partly through government persuasion, and partly through charitable donations from wealthy people or benevolent individuals, relief and attentions were extended, under various names, to helpless aged people, orphans, chaste widows and deformed and disabled persons.

Prior to and for some time after the arrival of the Japanese, however, this social work apparently fell into abeyance owing to internal turmoil and the unsettled state of things. Some years later, affairs in the island became more settled, so that the Government authorities could turn their attention to social service, and in fact they commenced making investigations with this end in view.

At this moment, the demise of the Empress Dowager Eisho took place, and in memory of the event the Emperor graciously made a grant to Taiwan as a fund for charity and relief work. Upon this, the Government of Taiwan issued an ordinance providing for charity hospital regulations and built charity hospitals in three different places, the Imperial donation being equitably allotted among the three institutions. The respective local governors were appointed directors of the hospitals, and they with one accord made efforts to expand the hospital operations and to augment their foundation capital. In the initial stage these hospitals accorded medical attention to limited classes of poor people, but at present they give gratuitous treatment to the needy class of people generally. Subsequently, with a view to providing against natural calamities and unexpected disaster, the Government promulgated the Taiwan Sufferers Relief Fund Regulations and forthwith put them in force, with the object of dealing with persons falling sick or dying on the public highways. As may be inferred from the above, the Government authorities are sparing no pains and are taking every possible occasion to frame plans for such matters, for instance, as the improvement of social conditions, reformatory, educational and relief work etc.

At present there are seven charitable institutions established at Taihoku, Shinchiku, Taichu, Kagi, Tainan, Takao and Mako; and there are in existence two charity fund corporations.

Social Reform Work

In former times, there were no regular markets in Taiwan worthy of the name. In those days, it was a usual thing that crowds of street-vendors should open their stalls at roadside corners or in temple grounds displaying pell-mell all their commodities – daily necessaries, fish, meat, vegetables and so on. The business transactions done in such a filthy manner presented a truly awful scene, a glance over which was more than enough to make any Japanese instantaneously sick.

In view of this, Viscount Goto, the then Chief of the civil Administration, conceived the idea of establishing a market under government supervision. Thanks to this intelligent policy, there are now to be found 180 public markets throughout the island. The benefits and conveniences thus enjoyed by the public cannot be estimated, to say nothing of the fact that they can buy the necessaries of life of good quality at low uniform prices.

Public Pawnshops

With the object of removing the long-established abuses attaching to private pawnshops and of securing low rates of interest to the needy class, the Government promulgated the Public Pawnshop Management Regulations in 1920, simultaneously opening one at Taihoku. There are at present established public pawnshops at Keelung, Taichu and Kagi besides that of Taihoku. Though it is not long since the enterprise was started, it has achieved a pronounced success as a financial benefit to the lower orders. It is no exaggeration to say that it decidedly forms an admirable line of modern social work.

Intelligence Office

In response to directions given by the authorities in 1921 as to the advisability of establishing intelligence offices for the relief of the unemployed, such offices have appeared in various places of importance. And there are indications of such establishments being increased in number.

Public Bath-houses, etc.

It was in the year 1905 that the first public bathhouse came into existence in Taiwan. The building was erected at Hokuto spring Resort at the expense of the Taiwan Ladies Charity Association and is still under the management of that body. In the year 1913, the Taihoku local Government constructed at Hokuto a large and magnificent public bath-house, the cost of construction of which was defrayed out of the public health fund. The establishment is called "Hokuto Kokyo Yokujo" and is largely used by the general public. The motives which actuated the authorities in taking this measure was to instruct the islanders in a cleanly custom and to inculcate sanitary ideas.

Amongst various other institutions, the following social reform activities that have come into existence may be mentioned public blocks of houses, tenement-houses for paupers, public boarding-houses, people's dining rooms, etc.

Social Protection and Culture Work

Numerous lines of enterprise coming under this denomination are fast engaging the attention of the Government and the public. Amongst activities of this kind so far started, the following are worthy of mention: Kindergartens, establishments for accommodating children of school age who are denied admission to school on account of their home surroundings; night schools for young working men; national language training associations; associations for guiding house-holders on practical common sense matters, good manners, current topics, spirit of self-government, sanitary ideas, civics, promotion of public interests etc.; associations of housewives; young men's associations; blind and deaf-mute schools; reform schools for depraved youths; establishments for giving protection to released prisoners. Above all, the national language training associations, the house-holders associations, the house-wives associations and the young men's associations are to be found in cities, towns and even in villages throughout the island, and are carrying on their work with remarkable success.

Bathing Establishment at Hokuto Spa

13

Scientific Research Work

In tropical colonies, there are found as a rule various institutions for carrying on scientific research in matters of tropical hygiene, tropical agriculture and tropical colonization; for instance, the Straits Settlements, the Federated Malay States, the Dutch East Indies, the Philippines and French Indo-China are no exceptions to the rule.

It scarcely needs to be said that such useful organs of scientific study have invariably made substantial contributions to the progress of science and human welfare. And this is the incentive that induced the Government of Taiwan in 1920 to found the Central Research Institute in Taihoku, bringing into the institute all kinds of scientific research work.

The Institute has for its chief aim the fundamental research and study of the subjects connected with the development of industrial enterprise and sanitary equipment in the island.

As regards the organization and function of this Institute, readers are for the sake of convenience referred to the diagram given below:

DEPARTMENT	SECTION
Agriculture	Plantation
	Agricultural chemistry
	Sugar industry
	Plant pathology
	Applied zoology
	Zootechny
Forestry	——
Industry	Chemical industry
	Electric chemistry
	Zymology
	General Purposes

There are branch laboratories of the Institute in eleven different localities in the island.

Libraries

The Government library was established in Taihoku in 1914. This is a well-stocked library, containing more than 45,000 volumes of Japanese, Chinese and European literature. The distinctive characteristic of this library is that it is provided with a large collection of rare and valuable books relating to South China. The latest figures available show that there are at present 14 libraries, public and private, in the island.

Museums

The erection of the Government museum in Taihoku dates as far back as 1908. The articles displayed comprise specimens of geology, mineralogy, zoology, history, and anthropology, including objects relating to the aborigines and many interesting ones relating to the South Sea Islands people. The number of specimens so far collected amounts to over 10,000. There are also two public museums in Tainan and Kagi, designed likewise for popular education.

Government Museum at Taihoku

The Government Commercial Museum

This commercial museum is under the immediate supervision of the Industrial Department, and is open to the interested public. The exhibits consist of commercial goods and specimens produced in Taiwan, Japan proper, South China and the South Sea Islands. A good stock of books and printed matter relative to all lines of commerce and trade is kept on the shelves. Inquiries and introductions concerning commercial transactions and designs for articles of commerce will be cordially attended to. In short, the aim of this establishment is to foster the development of commerce and trade and to impart commercial interest and knowledge to the public.

Appendix
Principal Cities, Famous Places, and Historic Sites

For the information of visitors to Taiwan, general descriptions of the leading cities, places of note and sites of historic interest are offered in the following pages.

Taihoku Province

Taihoku

Taihoku is the capital city of the island and the seat of the Government-General of Taiwan and the Government of Taihoku Province. The city limits cover an area of 6.7 square miles, with a population of 186,768 souls, including 51,717 Japanese, 122,922 Formosans and 12,129 foreign residents (mostly Chinese). The city of Taihoku is divided into three sections; namely, Jonai, Daitotei and Manka. With the establishment of a municipal system in 1920, many outlying districts have been incorporated into Greater Taihoku. Jonai, or Inner City, formerly encircled by the castle walls, was the capital city during the days of the Chinese regime. This forms the residential and business quarter for the large majority of the Japanese. Here and in the neighbourhood are found the important government offices, hospitals, schools, commercial establishments, banks, museums, library, hotels etc. The city has undergone a complete transformation since the advent of the Japanese, having witnessed great improvements and reconstruction in many and varied ways. It is well up to the standard of a modern civilized city.

Daitotei is situated to the north of Jonai and is chiefly inhabited by Formosans. When the limits of the port of Tamsui were extended up the Tamsui river to include Manka, this section became the centre of trade and commerce with China and foreign countries. This quarter has a reputation as a tea market. It is in this section that the leading business houses and foreign firms are to be found. Street improvements have been effected in the principal localities, and the quarter is now provided with the equipments and comforts of a modern city.

Manka lies close by the Tamsui river, west of Jonai. This is the oldest of the three sections. About 200 years ago, it had its flourishing days and active trade. But the river bed became shallower and shallower during the last half century and is no longer capable of affording facilities for the anchorage of ships. The result has been the gradual decay of trade and no traces of Manka's former prosperity are to be found today.

New Park

This park is laid out in modern style in the heart of the city proper. On account of its convenient and well-appointed situation many kinds of athletic exercises and open-air meetings take place here. The dense growth of luxuriant trees everywhere affords refreshing shade to children at play and holiday-makers.

The Museum

This magnificent structure towers up on the north side of the park, facing direct to the railway station. Many articles of scientific, historic and industrial interest are exhibited here. New-comers who wish to gain an idea of the island would do well in the first place to visit the museum.

The Botanical Garden

This garden lies in Nammoncho, embracing a comparatively large plot of ground. Here is located the Forestry Department of the Scientific Institute. The garden contains all sorts of tropical plants and flowers. Its hills, fountain, pond and other features form a picturesque landscape. To take a stroll in this garden is to enjoy something of the charming atmosphere of tropical nature.

Water-Works Reservoir, Taihoku

The Water-works Reservoir

The reservoir is situated on a hill, less than a couple of miles south of Taihoku. The waters pumped from the

Shinten River are filtered here and supplied to the city. This spot commands excellent views and at all seasons attracts many visitors.

Taiwan Jinsha

This celebrated Government shrine is situated at a point about two miles north of Taihoku. It is dedicated to the memory of H.I.H. the late Prince Kitashirakawa, who passed away in Taiwan during the expedition of 1895, and to the state deities of Japan. The sanctuary is constructed in an antique and elaborate style. All the year round, an endless stream of officials and townsfolk may be seen visiting the shrine for worship. The superbly beautiful views the precincts command, combined with the imposing sacred edifice, are well calculated to inspire feelings of reverence for the Divine.

Maruyama Park

A two miles' journey from Taihoku either by train or car takes one to this park. It lies on a hill facing the Taiwan shrine. In the grounds there is a zoological garden. To the east of Maruyama Park there lies a large sports ground which was laid out in April 1923, in commemoration of the visit of H.I.H. the Crown Prince of Japan.

Hokuto Hot Springs

This famed spa is situated half-way between Tamsui and Taihoku, seven miles distant from the latter place. It can be reached by train or by motor car. This district abounds in sulphur springs acknowledged to be efficacious for a variety of complaints. There is a grand public bath-house for the use of the general public. The hotels afford excellent accommodation, which, coupled with the charming scenery, attracts huge numbers of visitors, including many foreigners. This is really the best health resort in the whole island in respect of comfort and recreation. It may well be called the Hakone of Taiwan.

Sozan Hot Spring

This spot lies far back in the hills at a distance of nearly 7 miles from Shirin Station on the Tamsui line. The journey to this place can be made either by motor car, chair or rikisha. This resort was opened to the public at a recent date. But in point of quiet nature, rural charm, and the medical efficacy of its water, this spa can be favourable compared with Hokuto. On account of this, it is steadily becoming popular for spa-frequenters and holiday-makers. Persons fond of mountaineering may while away their time agreeably by climbing the hills in the neighbourhood.

Sozan Hot Spring Resort

Shinten

This a small country town, and is seven miles to the east of Taihoku. It lies on the bank of the Shinten River, and stands on the route to the Urai savage district, occupying an important position in the way of traffic and communication with the savage tribes of the interior. On the other side of the stream hang sheer wall-like cliffs presenting a picturesque scene with the deep blue water under their high precipices. There are tea-houses where one can rest and have light refreshments or more substantial food served. On summer days and evenings parties in search of coolness are seen visiting this resort.

Urai

Urai is a village, the nearest one to the city of Taihoku, the distance being some 17 miles. These erstwhile wild head-hunters had the first opportunity of being brought under the influence of modern civilization. They are now very orderly and are on friendly terms with both Japanese and Formosans. Here are a police station and a school for the aborigines' children. Here is also found a fine hot spring, and the mountain scenery is exceptionally beautiful. A pleasant day's trip can be made to this point from Taihoku.

Tamsui

Tamsui is an old seaport town situated at the terminus of the Tamsui branch line, 13 miles north of Taihoku. It contains a population of over 21,000. Before the Japanese took possession of this island, this port was well known and as thriving as Anping was in the South. The persistently accumulating bar, however, has rendered the harbour practically inaccessible to vessels. Especially since the progress of the harbour improvement works at Keelung, its importance has materially declined. The appearance of the town has not improved but the natural scenery is exceedingly beautiful. On a hill about one mile west of the station, there stand the remains of an old fort called "San Domingo," erected by the Spanish forces in 1629. On this site stands the British consulate. To the east of this site, there stands the compound of the Canadian Presbyterian Mission which was founded by the Rev. George Leslie Mackay, in 1872. Upon a table land not far from the old castle, there is a splendid golf course belonging to the Maiwan Golf Club.

Port of Tamsui

Keelung

This port is situated at the northern extremity of the island, on the shores of a deep gulf backed by a range of mountains which grace the port with striking scenery. It is at a distance of 18 miles from Taihoku and forms the starting point of the Trunk Line. The population is computed to be well over 56,000.

Keelung was once a Spanish settlement, but was subsequently captured and held by the Dutch, until they in turn gave place to the Chinese. The port was bombarded by the French under Admiral Lespès in August 1884, and was held by them until after the treaty of peace had been signed at Tientsin in June 1885.

Keelung, together with Takao, forms the main entrance to the island, affording, as it does, great facilities for transport and communication with Japan proper, South China and the South Seas. When the harbour extension works are completed, it will be possible to accommodate at the quay more than fifteen steamers of 3,000 to 10,000 tons. It can safely be said that even more flourishing and lively times than the present are well in view for the port.

In the vicinity of Keelung are found many rich coal mines and the famed gold mines of Zuiho and Kinkaseki. Keelung and neighbourhood being included in a strategic zone, it is strictly forbidden to photograph or sketch the features of land and sea.

On the eastern side of the port, there is the famous Courbet Beach, named after Admiral Courbet, who took command of the French fleet during the Franco-Chinese War. The monument that stands there was erected to the memory of the French officers and sailors who lost their lives on the field of honour.

Giran

Giran is a large and important town on the east coast, 47 miles distant from Keelung, with a population of over 21,000 souls. It is a town with a great future before it on account of the fertile plain stretching far around it and of the dense primeval forests on the savage border which produce large quantities of timber. This district was formerly a savage territory, but more than 130 years ago Chinese immigrants settled here, forming a town, and the savages were driven off into the mountains. The completion of the railway between Keelung and Suo will mean much for the future prosperity of the town.

Shokei Spa

This spa is situated five miles north of Giran on the railway line. This point commands a fine view of the Pacific Ocean across open paddy fields.

Suo

Suo is the starting point of the Giran Line and is within a five hours' voyage by coasting steamer from Keelung. The neighbouring mountain region produces marble and slate-stone. A carbonated spring which gushes forth in the vicinity, is used in the manufacture of mineral water.

Shinchiku Province

Shinchiku

Shinchiku is no insignificant city in North Taiwan, embracing a population of more than 36,000, and is the seat of the Provincial Government. More than two hundred years ago, the Chinese colonists, Holdos, as they were called, came over from south Fukien and formed a small colony, driving away the savages who were the original dwellers. Since then, this locality has grown up as a thriving business centre as well as a seat of Chinese learning. The surrounding districts are well known for the production of tea, rice, oranges and economic fibrous plants. In addition to this, Shinchiku is favoured with a fine healthful climate. This is all calculated to make the place still more prosperous.

Toyen

Toyen is situated 18 miles south of Taihoku and is one of the principal towns in North Taiwan, with a population of nearly 20,000. It is interesting to note that Toyen was, in direct contrast to Shinchiku, colonized three years later by the Chinese immigrants known as Hakkas from North Kwangtung Province. This town lies right in the centre of the tea and rice district, and forms an outlet for goods transported down from the distant savage borders. Toyen is the starting point for trips to Kappanzan and the wild savage districts of the interior.

Savage Huts

Kappanzan

Kappanzan is a well-reputed and very popular spot in the wild savage country. It is situated about 26 miles south-east of Toyen, forming a table land at an altitude of 1,400 feet above sea-level. It commands wonderful views of the Taikei river and of the thickly wooded green mountains around. In Kappanzan and the neighbouring mountain fastnesses there are found scattered groups of aborigines' huts where they evidently enjoy a contented life in close touch with Nature. Camphor is obtainable in large quantities in the forests around, and interested tourists may take advantage of their visit to inspect the camphor trees and camphor distilling-mills.

In a word, Kappanzan is one of the ideal spots in the island where one can obtain a good idea of savage life and wild mountain scenery, and of the enterprising operations being conducted by the Japanese for opening up the country and improving the condition of the ignorant savages. Excellent lodging accommodation can be obtained by special arrangement, at the Kihinkan, an elegant and indeed palatial building, and Kumpukan.

The whole journey there and back can be done by push-cars.

Taichu Province

Taichu

Taichu is the principal city in Central Taiwan, with a population reckoned at more than 38,000. It is situated 100 miles south of Taihoku and 99 miles north of Tainan. Within the city limits are located the Taichu Provincial Offce, the Municipal Offce, a lawcourt, hospitals, banks and many government buildings and important business establishments, including the Taiwan Newspaper Office.

It was once marked out by the Chinese Government as the administrative capital of the island. The construction of a castle was planned, but the choice was abandoned in favour of Taihoku. Immediately after the cession of the island to Japan, a new plan was made for the construction of a modern city. Taichu has since undergone great transformations, and the present streets are constructed on modern Japanese lines. Within a few minutes' walk from the station is Taichu Park, which is noted for its tasteful landscape gardening, with thickly growing trees, beautiful ponds and a picturesque watchtower. Situated in the region where rice, sugar and bananas are produced in large quantities, Taichu forms the central distribution market for these products.

The City of Taichu

Shoka

Shoka is an old Chinese town located on the trunk line, 12 miles south of Taichu, This is an important commercial centre for the Formosans in the South. The population is put at 18,000. Hakkeizan Hill commands a panoramic view of the town, and is celebrated for its association with the late Prince Kitashirakawa.

Rokko

Rokko is the oldest seaport town, situated 7 miles west of Shoka, with a population of over 30,000. Its commercial activity is not very great at the present time, but the manufacture of salt is very actively carried on.

Lake Candidius

Jitsugetsu-tan or Lake Candidius

The lake is so named after the pioneer Dutch missionary Georgius Candidius, who discovered it in 1627. It is also known as Suishako or Lake Dragon. It is located at a distance about 25 miles from Nisui Station, on the trunk line in Taichu Province. A private railway line is available from Nisui to Gaishatei, whence the journey may be continued either by tram car, push-car or chair.

The lake lies on an elevation some 2,400 feet above sea-level, surrounded by high mountain ranges from 5000 to 7,000 feet high, and has a circumference of about 10 miles. The beautiful expanse of calm, life-giving water presents the appearance of a vast mirror. The lake is made up of two parts shaped like sun and moon, as the name Jitsugetsutan signifies, having in the middle a little isle covered with beautiful woods.

At the east side of the lake, there is a village of a peculiar savage tribe known locally as water savages. They get their living by farming, fishing and hunting. They use long-shaped canoes of primitive construction on the lake. Each one is formed by hollowing out the trunk of a large tree, and is propelled by means of short, leaf-like paddles. The women of this tribe use very long pestles to pound millet and rice, as they do not use the mortar, and the crops are pounded on the ground.

Strange visitors are always warmly received by these people, especially when they are given some presents, say, in the form of saké or tobacco. On such occasion, the whole village people come out and charming young women begin singing with the accompaniment of rice pounding with their pestles. Their music is peculiarly interesting and is much admired.

According to their tradition, until a century and a half ago, their ancestors used to live in the high mountains near Kagi. One day they went out hunting, when they caught sight of a white deer which they chased into the deep mountain recesses where the poor creature suddenly left the track. Thus disappointed and fatigued, they wandered about the wild mountains aimlessly for three days, when they chanced to come across this beautiful lake. They thought that this lovely region was assigned them by Providence for their habitation, so they settled and stayed there

Now the trail of civilization has marched up to this secret recess of nature so that this spot has become a centre of general interest. With a view to centralizing at this point all the electric plants in the island, the Taiwan Electric Power Company has undertaken operations on a large scale. Their scheme is to produce 140,000 h.p. hydraulic power by utilizing the lake water. When this huge work is finished, the whole island will be supplied with light and power. For many reasons, this locality has a at great future before it.

The lake-side hotel "Kampekiro" is worth stopping overnight.

Lake Candidius Savages

Horigai

Wending one's way a few miles to the northeast from the lake, one will come to a town situated on an open plateau. This is Horigai. Hori and the adjacent district afford a splendid hunting ground for naturalists to collect wonderful varieties of insects and reptiles, and butterflies in particular. Large orders for these are coming in from many quarters of the world.

Musha

Musha is a savage village situated at an elevation of 4,000 feet above sea-level, about 16 miles east of Horigai, which distance can be covered by push-car. Here one will enjoy the prospect of the central range of high mountains soaring up into the skies. It will be interesting to note that the climate and flora at this altitude are almost the same as those of Japan in the spring season.

The savage tribes inhabiting this district used to be very wild and fierce head-hunters before they submitted to Japanese authority.

Our remarks here would not be complete without mentioning one thing more for the information of mountain-climbers, explorers and students of natural science; that is, that a transverse path has been opened up to Karenko from Musha across the central back-bone of the mountains. The distance covers approximately 56 miles. The attempt to travel this path presupposes previous good arrangements with the police authorities.

Mt. Niitaka

Niitaka-yama (Mt. Morrison)

Mt. Niitaka, the crowning glory of Taiwan, stands in the central mountain range under the Tropic of Cancer. Rising to a height of 13,075 feet above sea-level, it distinctly exceeds in altitude Mt. Fuji, the sacred highest mountain in Japan proper. Among foreigners, it is better known as Mt. Morrison, being so named after the captain of a British steamer that called at Anping. The appellation "Niitakayama" which means "New High Mountain" was given it by the late Emperor Meiji. Though it out-vies Fujisan in height, it can hardly match Fuji in grandeur and beauty.

The slopes of Mt. Niitaka for upwards of 6,000 feet are thickly clothed with evergreen groves and primeval forests. Orchids, lilies, trailing plants, Chamaecyparis obtusa, C. Pisifera, Cryptomerias, Camphor trees, etc., are found growing and flourishing there in the restful lap of Mother Nature, tinting the mountains with rich colouring.

Niitakayama consists of three majestic peaks, which truly command a grand view of the whole island and the great seas around. These mountain tops are snow-capped for a good part of the year.

The ascent of Niitaka-yama should be attempted only in October or November, April or May, owing to summer rains swelling the mountain rivers. Up to recent years, few have climbed up Niitaka-yama, not only on account of the danger due to the route being infested by savages, but also because of the great expense of the trip, which cannot be undertaken without a large party of Japanese patrols and native porters. A splendid path leading out to Tamazato on the east coast across the central range from Shushu having been opened up, however, it has now become much easier for intending travellers to make the ascent of the mountain from either point. The trip would best be started from Nisui on the trunk line, and all the necessary arrangements for the ascent should be made at Shushu.

Tainan Province

Tainan

Tainan is situated 200 miles south of Keelung and is the oldest and second largest city in the island, with a population of over 83,000. In the Chinese days, it was for two centuries the capital of the island, known as Taiwan-fu. While Taiwan was under the rule of the Dutch and General Koxinga, this was also made the headquarters of the whole island. Under the Chinese administration, the city enjoyed great prosperity as the centre of political, commercial and industrial activity and of learning as well. Since the administrative seat was removed to Taihoku, the importance of Tainan has been chiefly commercial. The old Chinese walls, some five miles in circumference, have been pulled down and the gates removed for the passage of the railway and new modern roads.

When the city was organized as a municipality, the port of Anping was annexed, the area constituting the whole municipality being about 15 square miles. In the city are situated the Tainan Provincial Government Office, the City Office, the South Garrison Headquarters, the Law Court, hospitals, schools, the Tainan Newspaper Office, and branches of important commercial firms.

The city and neighbourhood abound in places of interest and relics with historic, associations, which are kept in good condition and well preserved.

Tainan-Jinsha

This is the celebrated shrine of H.I.H. the late Prince

Kitashirakawa, who fell a victim to a malignant malarial fever during the Japanese expedition in 1895. The shrine precincts mark the exact spot where the Prince fixed his quarters on the eve of his impending demise.

Kaizan-Jinsha

This is a shrine dedicated by the Formosans to the spirit of Koxinga, a celebrated loyalist of the last days of the Ming Dynasty, who came over to this island, and drove out the Dutch settlers.

Confucius Temple

This is the largest and most important temple of the kind in all the island. It was erected some 250 years ago.

Tainan Park

Sekikanro

This structure, otherwise called "Fort Provintia", was constructed and occupied by the Dutch in 1624 on an elevation. Through repeated repairs, its original shape is now substantially altered.

Tainan Park

This is well worth visiting as it is excellently laid out on a grand scale, and is of practical utility and noted for its varied tropical plants and flowers.

Shinro

Here is located the headquarters of the English Presbyterian Mission, first established by Dr. Maxwell in 1865.

Fort Zeelandia

Anping

This port is the oldest in the South, and lies two miles and a half west of Tainan, connected with the city by a trolly line or motor car. The port itself is but an open roadstead, vessels anchoring almost two miles off the beach. Passengers and goods are conveyed between land and sea by lighters and peculiar bamboo catamarans or "Teppai" as they are locally called. It was formerly a thriving port, but with the progress of harbour construction work at Takao, its importance has correspondingly declined. In Anping there remain the ruins of "Fort Zeelandia", now called Sekkan-jo, which preserve the memory of Dutch rule in the island. The fort was besieged and eventually captured by Koxinga in 1662. On the foreshore of Anping, there is a large salt refinery.

Catamarans or Teppai

Kagi

Kagi is situated 182 miles south of Keelung and 47 miles north of Takao. It is next to Tainan, the largest city in South Taiwan, containing a population of upward of 42,000. It is well provided with means of communication, electric and water supply works, All the varied equipment requisite for modern city life is in process of acquirement. The Government railway to Mt. Arisan starts from this point and the place has good connections by private light railways with the sugar producing centres. And the headquarters of the well-known Kanan Irrigation Works Corporation is located here.

The saw-mills of the Arisan Forest Exploitation Department certainly form an interesting object, and are well worth visiting. The plant is built on a big scale, well equipped with machines of the latest type. Quantities of logs brought down from the mountains are handled and converted into all shapes of timber by the machines before one's eyes; a spectacular scene, which should not be missed.

Kanshirei Hot Spring

Kanshirei spa is a noted health resort in South Taiwan, situated almost eleven miles east of Koheki Station. The journey can be done by motor car or push-car. In respect of natural beauty and of comfortable accommodation, it will bear comparison with Hokuto in North Taiwan.

Tropic of Cancer Indication Tower

This tower stands a few miles south of Kagi.

Go-Ho Temple

This temple is situated at a place called Chuhosho, about eight miles to the south-east of Kagi. It is erected to the memory of the celebrated humanistic martyr Go-Ho. The story of the hero is so beautiful and pathetically interesting that it is always related as a moral tale among Formosan homes.

The hero in question saw the light near Kagi nearly two hundred years ago. As a child he frequently visited the Arisan savage border, accompanied by his father, for bartering with the wild hill-men. On account of the thorough knowledge of their language and their ways of living he acquired, he was appointed as official interpreter to deal with the people. As a matter of course, he soon won their feelings and was highly respected as their master. They all submitted to his rule, heart and soul. Notwithstanding his many years' assiduous efforts in their behalf, he found it impossible to make them forego their evil practice of head-hunting. Finally overcome by keen regret, he resolved to break off their habit at the sacrifice of his own life. One day Go-Ho told his savage friends that the following morning when they went out on their head-hunting expedition, they might came across an old man dressed in red whom they could behead with impunity. The ignorant savages acted as they were told, but they were struck dumb with astonishment when they found that the very victim offered was none but their affectionate old friend. This noble act was just what was needed to bring home to the brutal savages a sense of crime and sin, and thereafter the Arisan tribesmen absolutely abandoned their superstitious practice.

It is a tradition handed down among the Arisan savages that after his dramatic death the spirit of Go-Ho haunts their habitations to see if they are behaving righteously.

The late Count General Sakuma, one of the former Governors-General, who took a great interest in the control and enlightenment of the wild savages, visited this temple and presented a tablet of his own hand-writing in appreciation of Go-Ho's beautiful act of self-sacrifice.

Maso Temple

This Chinese temple is situated in a country town called Hokko about 11 miles north-west of Kagi. This town is largely indebted to the temple for its constantly increasing prosperity and its active life. Half a million of pilgrims resort annually to the Maso temple from all corners of the island, chiefly in winter and spring. The deity enshrined there is worshipped as the protector of fields, harvests, navigation and warfare. The temple buildings are gorgeous, and magnificently planned in characteristic Chinese style.

Takao Province

Takao

Takao is the capital city of Takao Province, and forms the terminus of the trunk line. It is situated at a distance of 249 miles from Keelung, its population being estimated at almost 40,000. This port was opened to foreign trade 66 years ago, at the same time as the other Taiwan ports. This port is as important and flourishing as that of Keelung in the North. The harbour construction work is making headway, and a great future is assured for this port.

The chain of hills stretching northward from the harbour afford charming prospects and the views along the harbour mouth are wonderful. A remarkable increase in the exports of sugar, rice and other commodities, and the frequent calls of many big steamers of different nationalities, have apparently given new life to the port. On the other hand, Takao is steadily growing up as an industrial centre with the establishment of a cement factory, a manure manufacturing company, soda works and so on.

From Takao, a government branch line of 15 miles runs as far as Heito via Hozan, through a district devoted to the cultivation of sugar and rice.

The River Shimo Tansuikei

This is the largest river in the island, taking its source in the streams of the Niitaka range, and running through the plain of Heito. The railway bridge spanning the river extends 5,007 feet in length and ranks as the longest in the East. It is one of the great sights to be witnessed by travellers in Taiwan.

On the southern bank of the river stands the police aerodrome.

Shimo Tamsui-Kei Bridge

Heito

Heito is a town of growing importance in the southern district, embracing a population of 24,000. At this point light railways branch off in many directions. The Heito plain produces large quantities of rice and sugar, and here can be witnessed the characteristic aspects of the tropic zone. The Heito Factory of the Taiwan Seito Kaisha (Taiwan Sugar Company) is on a grand scale and has perfect equipment. A visit to this mill is usually included in the itinerary of tourists travelling to the South.

Koshun

Koshun is a town in the southern extremity of the island,

more than 65 miles distant from Takao, with a population of 11,000 inhabitants. The climate of this region is delightful and springlike all the year round, as the name Koshun signifies.

The champaign district around here was in olden times inhabited by savages, but is now being brought under civilization by the Japanese. At points not far from Koshun are located the Live-Stock Farming Station, the Tropical Plants Nursery, and Shujukei hot springs.

Garambi Lighthouse

This famous lighthouse stands at the southernmost cape. In former days, the savage tribes in the southern district were extremely wild, and warlike against strange comers. On many occasions, sailors belonging to foreign ships wrecked in the neighbouring waters were taken prisoners and ruthlessly massacred instead of being received as sufferers.

In 1871, a large fishing and trading vessel of the Loochoans was wrecked on the southern coast, when fifty-four of the crew were murdered by the savages of the Botan tribe. In 1867, the American barque *Rover* ran on a sunken rock, as a consequence of a severe gale, far south of Takao, and her people met with a similar fate at the hands of the Kualu savages.

Light House at Garambi

In compliance with a strong demand made by the American Government in the interest of all foreign vessels navigating on the southern coast, the Chinese authorities constructed a light-house in 1882 at the cape of Garambi, and this was reconstructed by the Japanese Government in 1897 at a cost of 68,000 yen. Towering up to a height of 180 feet above high-water mark, and with a light strong enough to be visible at a distance of 20 knots, this structure stands out as a conspicuous figure amidst the roaring billows.

Bokoto or the Pescadores

Bokoto is an archipelago consisting of upwards of 60 islands, lying 25 miles west of the main island, and dotted about the Tropic of Cancer. The surface, mainly of sandstone formation, is flat and the soil sterile. The violent north-east wind blowing for half the year, and the typhoons which exert their full fury in the Pescadores Channel, prevent the growth of trees and cause frequent shipwrecks.

The supply of wood and water is naturally very scarce,

and fishing is the principal resource of the inhabitants. In farming, millet, peanuts and sweet-potatoes are the principal items. The whole population is estimated at fifty thousand, the bulk of the inhabitants being fishermen, whence the Spanish name of the archipelago has passed into general European usage.

In respect of historic associations, the Pescadores are full of interest. Some centuries ago, the Pescadores used to be the base of operations for Japanese and Chinese piratical traders and were occupied alternately by the Chinese, the Dutch, Koxinga, the French, and the Chinese, until they passed into the possession of Japan together with the main island.

Port Mako

Mako, with a population of 25,000, is the only natural harbour in the island groups. Its deep water provides a good anchorage for vessels, and affords a haven of refuge when severe storms are encountered in this part of the Formosan Channel. Mako is situated within a voyage of eight and ten hours from Anping and Takao respectively. The town is encircled by an old fortification with towers erected at important points; the whole thing viewed from a distant sea looks like a sea-nymph's palaces. Within, and in the vicinity of, the town are the District Office, the Fortress Commandant Headquarters, and the Secondary Naval Station.

Among places of historic interest, is a monument erected to the memory of Admiral Courbet, who met a deplorable death here, succumbing to cholera during the Franco-Chinese campaign of 1884.

East Coast

As can be seen from the map inserted in this book, the central mountain range extends far towards the eastern coast, leaving only a belt of open land. On the northern part of the east coast, there stretches a continuation of high cliffs for almost twenty-five miles, perpendicularly rising in places sheer six thousand feet, and abruptly dropping deep down where the waters of the boundless Pacific lap the solitary crags beneath. These are said to be the highest and most magnificent sea-cliffs known in the world. These precipitous mountains are clothed from base to summit with all sorts of trees, shrubs and grasses, growing in a most luxuriant manner; and the gigantic wall of rocks is riven every few miles by huge gorges of unique grandeur. It is a pity that owing to the remote situation of this natural scenery and to the lack of adequate facilities of communication, few persons have had the opportunity of witnessing these beautiful creations of Nature.

On account of this physical formation, there is practically no anchorage anywhere on the east coast.

From the very earliest days, the mountain district and plains in the east coast were occupied by the Tayal, Ami and Piyuma tribes of aborigines, the Amis possessing the richest and most attractive country. The Piyuma and Ami groups mostly consist of the so-called domesticated savages. Influenced by the superior strength and intelligence of the new comers from South China, they have adopted the customs and speech of the Chinese and have further betaken themselves to farming. Fortunately their struggles for existence with the Chinese settlers has not been so severe as in the western plain, so they remained in undisputed possession of their home land. Matters standing thus, the eastern districts of the island, containing many possibilities and resources for economic development,

A Cliff on the East Coast

remained closed to the advance of civilization and the enterprising operations of progressive colonists. This was the case even after the arrival of the Japanese in the island, as they found their hands full of affairs that urgently demanded their attention elsewhere. A good many years later the time became ripe for the Japanese to set about opening up the sealed-up country of the east, and thanks to their strenuous efforts, there have sprung up industrial enterprises in various parts which evidently afford bright prospects for the welfare and prosperity of this backward region.

Some day when the Taito–Karenko railway line which is now nearing completion may be extended and connected with points in the western coast, then an amazing change would come over the eastern coast so far as regards its industrial and commercial development.

Sea-Shore, Taito

Taito Province

Taito

Taito is a town situated at the mouth of the Pinan River, with a population of 8,200 souls, including that of the neighbouring district. The sea is usually rough along the coast except in the summer months, and a landing is effected through the surf with the assistance of expert savages.

In the early days of the Japanese occupation, the Heito plain which stretches out between the central mountain mass and the coastal range was apparently a vast wild land under the domination of sparse savage tribesmen.

Since the Taito Exploitation Company and the Taito Sugar Manufacturing Company were established, thousands of acres of land that had been left untouched have been brought under cultivation. With the cooperation of the Government, the Taito Exploitation Company is now carrying on extensive water utilization works. The completion of the undertaking will have a great effect in increasing the production of rice in the Taito plain.

Kotosho or Botel Tobago Island

This is a little-known solitary isle inhabited by the most primitive aboriginal people. It is situated at a distance of some 49 miles from Taito, and has a circumference of 30 miles. A single chain of hills penetrates the island longitudinally from which small streams flow out into the sea. The climate is hot at all seasons; however, owing to the abundance of the rainfall and constant sea breezes, the temperature is kept at a moderate level. The water-taro, dry taro, sweet-potato, and little millet are grown; goats, peculiar pigs, fish, chicken and coconuts are abundant, so that the islanders are well supplied with articles of diet. Unlike other savage tribes, they are not addicted to the use of intoxicating drink or tobacco. The men, as a rule, go almost naked, but the women wear a sleeveless coat made of hemp-fibres and banana-leaves. They are most simple and gentle, yet very timid and superstitious, and are strikingly different from other tribesmen in customs and traditions. On account of the frequent visitations of violent storms and terrific tropical downpours, their dwellings are of singularly complicated construction. Their canoes are built with beautiful designs and decorations that unquestionably call for notice. They are clever carvers of wood, and manufacture earthenware pots and clay figures. They like, and in fact highly value, silver coins, with which they make many sorts of ornaments. Experts say that they speak the same dialect as the people of Batan Island in the Philippines and that there is evidence to show that the Malay element, somewhat mixed with the Papuan, predominates among the savages. It is therefore very likely that their ancestors migrated from the South Sea Islands, driven by the current or by high winds.

They are the sole occupants of the island. The island population numbers about 2,070, the only Japanese living there being a few policemen. These strange islanders would certainly be interesting to travellers, and to scientists in particular.

Botel Tobago

Kashoto or Samasana Island

This is another little-known islet, situated 18 miles off Taito. The inhabitants mainly consist of fishermen who have emigrated from South China, and are reckoned at 1,600 in number. Here is established the Government Vagabonds Reformatory.

Karenko Province

Karenko

Karenko lies on the north-east coast, 94 knots southward from Keelung, and the two ports are connected by regular steamer services.

Karenko's position makes it as an important seaport, as in the case of Taito, both being gateways to the eastern part of Taiwan. The sea is usually high, especially when the strong north-east monsoon prevails during the winter months. At such times the landing of cargo and passengers through the surf is too dangerous an enterprise to undertake.

Up to fifteen years ago, this place was but a small and insignificant village bordering on the savage frontier. With the establishment of a local government here in 1910, however, agricultural, forestry and mineral working enterprises have been started, and the immigration of Japanese farmers, the subjugation of the savage people, and the railway construction scheme have been achieved with good success.

As a result of these favourable plans, the little town has steadily grown up so that it has now assumed the features of quite a modern city with a great future before it. It already possesses a population of over 7,000 inhabitants.

The anticipated completion in the course of 1925 of

the railway line down to Taito will assuredly add much importance to Karenko as a commercial locality.

List of place names with modern equivalents

Most of the places in this book have different names today. This list of place names includes the modern equivalents in both Chinese characters and common English or romanized spellings.

Anping	安平	Anping
Arisan	阿里山	Alishan
Bokoto	澎湖	Penghu/Pescadores
Chuhosho	中埔	Zhongpu
Gaishatei	車埕	Checheng
Garambi	鵝鑾鼻	Eluanbi/Oluanpi
Giran	宜蘭	Yilan
Go-Ho Temple	吳鳳廟	Wu-Feng Temple
Heito	屏東	Pingtung
Hokko	北港	Beigang
Hokuto	北投	Beitou
Horigai	埔里	Puli
Hozan	鳳山	Fengshan
Jitsugetsu-tan	日月潭	Zintun/ Sun Moon Lake
Kagi	嘉義	Chiayi
Kanshirei	關子嶺	Guanziling
Kappanzan	角板山	Jiaoban Shan

Karenko	花蓮	Hualien
Kashoto	綠島	Green Island
Keelung	基隆	Keelung
Koheki	後壁	Houbi
Koshun	恆春	Hengchun
Kotosho	蘭嶼	Ponso no Tao/ Orchid Island
Mako	馬公	Magong
Maruyuma Park	台北動物園	Taipei Zoo
Maso Temple	北港朝天宮	Chaotian Temple, Beigang
Musha	霧社	Wushe
Niitaka-yama	玉山	Jade Mountain/ Yu Shan
Nisui	二水	Ershui
Rokko	鹿港	Lukang
Sekikanro	赤崁樓	Fort Provintia
Sekkan-jo	安平古堡	Fort Zeelandia
Shinchiku	新竹	Hsinchu
Shinro	新樓醫院	Sinlau Hospital
Shinten	新店	Xindian
Shoka	彰化	Changhua
Shokei	礁溪	Jiaoxi
Suishako	see *Jitsugetsu-tan*	
Suo	蘇澳	Su'ao
Taichu	台中	Taichung
Taihoku	台北	Taipei
Tainan	台南	Tainan
Taito	台東	Taitung
Takao	高雄	Kaohsiung
Tamsui	淡水	Tamsui/Danshui
Toyen	桃園	Taoyuan
Urai	烏來	Ulay/Wulai

Units of Measurement

Japanese units of measurement are used throughout. Here is a list with metric, US, and Imperial equivalents.

Japanese	Metric	US	Imperial
Chobu	0.99 ha	2.45 acres	2.45 acres
Kin	600 g	1.323 lb	1.323 lb
Koku	180.4 l	47.65 gal	39.68 gal
Tsubo	3.31 m^2	35.58 sq ft	35.58 sq ft

Lightning Source UK Ltd.
Milton Keynes UK
UKHW020143230422
401939UK00009B/468/J

9 781788 692694